GOING TO COURT

GOING TO COURT

AN INTRODUCTION TO THE
U.S. JUSTICE SYSTEM

Ursula Furi-Perry

Printed in the United States of America

17 16 15 14 13   5 4 3 2 1

Library of Congress Cataloging-in-Publication Data

Furi-Perry, Ursula, author.
  Going to court : an introduction to the U.S. justice system / Ursula Furi-Perry.
      pages cm
  Includes index.
  ISBN 978-1-62722-620-2 (alk. paper)
  1. Procedure (Law)--United States--Juvenile literature. 2. Due process of law--United States--Juvenile literature. 3. Criminal justice, Administration of--United States--Juvenile literature. I. Title.
  KF8841.F87 2014
  347.73'5--dc23

                                2014033820

ISBN 978-1-62722-023-1

CONTENTS

INTRODUCTION

Welcome to *Going to Court: How Trials Work*! This book is a look at the U.S. justice system, how our disputes are resolved, and the rights and duties that all U.S. citizens possess.

In the United States, a trial is the most common way to solve legal disputes that people or institutions cannot settle, or resolve, by themselves. The chief purpose of a trial is to secure the fair administration of justice between the people involved, whether they are having a disagreement or someone is accused of committing a crime. A trial tries to find the truth of the dispute and apply the law to it.

The two major types of trials in the United States are civil trials and criminal trials. Civil trials are held to settle disagreements between two parties, usually individuals or businesses. These are noncriminal disputes, such as divorce proceedings, disagreements between landlords and tenants, and other lawsuits. The U.S. court system sees and helps resolve many cases that deal with disagreements or disputes between private parties every year. The court system also makes sure the wronged person in the situation is given justice, usually in the form of an amount of money the other party has to pay him or her.

In a criminal trial, a person charged with a crime is found guilty or not guilty and, if found guilty, sentenced to a punishment. In these trials, the government is actually bringing the case to trial on behalf of the citizens, to punish someone for breaking the law. Criminal law keeps people from putting the health, safety, and welfare of citizens in danger.

Criminal trials are about punishing someone for committing a crime. These are covered in Part 1 of this book. Civil trials are about solving a problem between two parties, and they are discussed in Part 2 of this book. But first, let's look at how the court system is set up and where our laws come from.

The American Court System

Cases are decided at different levels of courts. The U.S. courts operate within a federalist system. **Federalism** describes a system of government in which power is purposely divided so that no one state, person, or governing body has too much power. In our nation, there is a central unit, called the federal government. The **federal government** is composed of three distinct branches: legislative, executive, and judicial. The **legislative branch** has the power to create, amend, or repeal laws. The **executive branch** is headed by the President of the United States and enforces the laws. Finally, the **judicial branch** interprets the laws and applies them to individual cases. The Supreme Court is the highest court in the country, and it is the court of **final appeal**, meaning that it is the very last place you can try a legal case after trying it in the lower courts, and after that it is decided for good.

Underneath the federal government are individual state and local governments. Each of the 50 states gets to make and enforce its own laws. Each city gets to make and enforce its own local laws. Of course, all states and local units (also called municipalities) must work within the bounds of the federal government.

Both the federal government and the various state governments have their own court systems. Federal courts can hear cases that involve federal crimes. For example, many drug and weapon possession offenses are federal crimes, so a **defendant** who is accused of one of those crimes may be brought into a federal court. The case begins in the District Court, which is the trial-level court.

The Three Branches of U.S. Government

- Legislative: Makes the laws
- Executive: Enforces the laws
- Judicial: Applies the laws

From there, a case can be appealed to the Courts of Appeals, also known as the Circuit Courts. An **appeal** is when someone who loses a case in a trial court asks a higher court (the appellate court) to review the trial court's decision. After an appellate decision, if the person is still dissatisfied with the **verdict**—the court's decision—then he or she may ask the U.S. Supreme Court to hear the case. However, it is very rare for the Supreme Court to hear cases. From

the many thousands of cases presented to it each year, the Supreme Court only hears a select few. Typically, only a criminal defendant may appeal a case; unless some sort of procedural error occurred, meaning that the rules of the court were broken, the prosecution will not be able to appeal the case.

Appeals help protect people who have been wrongly convicted of a crime in a lower court. They can also help the **prosecution**—the lawyer who is trying to prove the case against someone accused of a crime—have a second chance to convict the person if the rules of the court were broken during the trial. The prosecution, however, always has to avoid **double jeopardy** when they appeal: That means a defendant cannot be tried again on the same charges following a legitimate acquittal or conviction, in which the rules of the court were followed.

Levels of Federal Courts

U.S. Supreme Court

↓

Courts of Appeals/ Circuit Courts

↓

District Courts

Courts operate at the state and local levels as well. Many crimes are state crimes, meaning they are subject to the laws of the state where the crime occurred: for example, murder or battery of another person. Each state has its own set of criminal laws. Some laws set forth what constitutes a crime. Other laws provide for the appropriate penalties and punishments for those who have been convicted of a crime. Still other laws provide for defenses to criminal **culpability**: This means there are established paths to follow that can keep a defendant from deserving blame. For instance, you may be able to prove that you are not to blame by presenting **evidence**—information, documents, or objects that establish facts—that you acted in self-defense.

Under the U.S. **Constitution**, both criminally accused people and people involved in civil disputes have the right to have their day in court: They may try their cases under our **adversarial** system of justice, meaning that the people involved in a dispute have the responsibility for finding and presenting evidence. An **impartial** party—the judge or jury, who do not favor one side or the other before the trial begins—will decide the case.

Laws

Our legal system relies heavily on past **precedent**. This means that courts look at cases that were previously decided when analyzing a new case. The courts resolve cases with similar facts in the same way as past precedent—the case that came before—was resolved.

For example, let's say a previous case decided that a defendant was guilty of shoplifting when he put a necklace in his pocket and was apprehended by the police as he tried to leave the store. In a new case, where a new defendant put a bracelet in his pocket and then tried to leave the store, that new defendant is also likely to be found guilty. The facts of the two cases are similar enough to be easily compared, and therefore the precedent case will apply.

Some cases are so new, or deal with such novel issues, that no precedent is available for the courts to use. For example, a criminal defendant might have a case dealing with cyber-bullying on a social media website. If no similar cases have already been decided in the defendant's state, then the court might do several things:

- It might look at cases dealing with similar issues that have been decided by the same court—in this example, perhaps cases dealing with bullying in school.

- It might look to other states where courts have decided similar cases.

- It might set completely new precedent regarding the new issue.

Legal authority is followed by the courts when deciding cases: It is how the courts know they are following the established laws of the state and country. Both common law and enacted law play an important part in the American system of justice and deciding individual cases. **Common laws** come from tradition and judge's opinions rather than laws themselves; they are made up of formal statements from judges and courts on how they decided a case and what principles of the law they used. **Enacted laws** have been formally adopted by state or federal legislature. They include constitutions, **statutes**, **ordinances**, and regulations.

PART
1

CRIMINAL
TRIALS

Chapters 1–13

Chapter 1

AN OVERVIEW OF THE CRIMINAL PROCESS

- Key Personnel in Criminal Trials
- The Purposes of Criminal Law
- The Criminal Process from Arrest to Appeal

A criminal case in court begins when the prosecution (the government) brings charges against the defendant (an individual who is accused of a crime).

Key Personnel in Criminal Trials

In the courtroom, a **judge**, who oversees the trial and resolves any issues that arise based on the law, is typically present. Judges are employed by the court, the judicial branch of the government. The defense often has the right to decide whether a case will be tried by a judge or jury, but in some states or other **jurisdictions** (legal territories) both the prosecution and the defense have the right to demand a jury

A Judge oversees the trial and resolves any issues that arise. Judges are employed by the court

People in the Court

- Judge
- Jury
- Prosecutor
- Defense Attorney
- Defendant
- Bailiff
- Court Clerk
- Court Reporter

trial. The **jury** consists of 12 persons in serious felony cases, but some states allow for as few as six-person juries in less serious misdemeanor cases. The jury is made up of other citizens from the defendant's community. The jury considers various issues based on the facts of the case and decides if the defendant is guilty or not guilty.

A court contains various other people who work in the courthouse. A **court clerk** assists with filings and documentation. A **court reporter** or stenographer records the trial in writing. A **bailiff** may be present to help keep order during the litigation proceedings.

Attorneys represent both sides in the criminal process. The attorneys who represent the government are called **prosecutors**, and they may also be called Assistant District Attorneys or Deputy District Attorneys. The role of the prosecutor is to prove beyond a reasonable doubt that the defendant committed every element of the crime with which he or she is charged.

The attorneys who represent the criminal defendant are called **defense attorneys**. The role of the defense attorney is to (1) disprove the prosecution's case, (2) show that the defendant did not commit the **alleged** (unproven) crime, or (3) show that the defendant had a proper defense or reason for committing the alleged crime.

The Purposes of Criminal Law

There are several purposes to having a body of law in place to govern criminal conduct, including the following:

- **Punishment:** To impose penalties, such as fines and jail time, which seek to punish those who engage in criminal conduct

- **Deterrence and prevention:** To prevent criminals and others from engaging in criminal conduct

- **Rehabilitation and reform:** To provide the criminal offender with the opportunity to make good

- **Protection of the accused:** To provide the criminal defendant with rights and procedural safeguards

- **Redress and protection of the victims and community:** To provide victims of crime with the opportunity to receive justice for the crimes committed against them

The Criminal Process from Arrest to Appeal

Here is a helpful resource from the Victims of Crime website (http://www.victimsofcrime. org/help-for-crime-victims/get-help -bulletins-for-crime-victims/the-criminal -justice-system) that provides an overview describing the criminal justice system.

The Criminal Justice System: What Is It?

The criminal justice system is the set of agencies and processes established by governments to control crime and impose penalties on those who violate laws. There is no single criminal justice system in the United States but rather many similar, individual systems. How the criminal justice system works in each area depends on the jurisdiction that is in charge: city, county, state, federal or tribal government or military installation. Different jurisdictions have different laws, agencies, and ways of managing criminal justice processes. The main systems are:

- **State:** State criminal justice systems handle crimes committed within their state boundaries.

- **Federal:** The federal criminal justice system handles crimes committed on federal property or in more than one state.

System Components

Most criminal justice systems have five components—law enforcement, prosecution, defense attorneys, courts, and corrections, each playing a key role in the criminal justice process.

- **Law Enforcement:** Law enforcement officers take reports for crimes that happen in their areas. Officers investigate crimes and gather and protect evidence. Law enforcement officers may arrest offenders, give testimony during the court process, and conduct follow-up investigations if needed.

- **Prosecution:** Prosecutors are lawyers who represent the state or federal government (not the victim) throughout the court process—from the first appearance of the accused in court until the accused is acquitted or sentenced. Prosecutors review the evidence brought to them by law enforcement to decide whether to file charges or drop the case. Prosecutors present evidence in court, question witnesses, and decide (at any point after charges have been filed) whether to negotiate plea bargains with defendants. They have great discretion, or freedom, to make choices about how to prosecute the case. Victims may contact the prosecutor's office to find out which prosecutor is in charge of their case, to inform the prosecutor if the defense attorney has contacted the victim, and to seek other information about the case.

- **Defense Attorneys:** Defense attorneys defend the accused against the government's case. They are ether hired by the defendant or (for defendants who cannot afford an attorney) they are assigned by the court. While the prosecutor represents the state, the defense attorney represents the defendant.

- **Courts:** Courts are run by judges, whose role is to make sure the law is followed and oversee what happens in court. They decide whether to release offenders before the trial. Judges accept or reject plea agreements, oversee trials, and sentence convicted offenders.

Witnesses are the people who saw an event, such as a crime or an accident, take place. They provide **testimony**—a formal written or spoken statement—in court about what they saw.

- **Corrections:** Corrections officers supervise convicted offenders when they are in jail, in prison, or in the community on probation or parole. In some communities, corrections officers prepare pre-sentencing reports with extensive background information about the offender to help judges decide sentences. The job of corrections officers is to make sure the facilities that hold offenders are secure and safe. They oversee the day-to-day custody of inmates. They also oversee the release processes for inmates and sometimes notify victims of changes in the offender's status.

In the next chapters, you will read in more detail about crimes, defenses to crimes, criminal protections, and the criminal process.

Discussion Questions

1. Discuss the many purposes of criminal law.

2. How does precedence work? Why do courts use it?

Writing Prompts

1. Why is it important to have fundamental rights guaranteed to citizens? Why is it important to have a Bill of Rights, which guarantees those fundamental rights?

_____

_____

_____

_____

2. If you were an attorney involved in a criminal case, would you rather represent the prosecution or the defense? Explain why.

_____

_____

_____

_____

Chapter 2

ESSENTIAL ELEMENTS OF CRIMES

- Mens Rea: Intent
- Actus Reus: Action
- The Burden of Proof
- The Standard of Proof
- Felonies and Misdemeanors

In order to prove that the defendant is guilty of the crime charged, the prosecution must prove certain essential elements. Elements are part of the rules of court—in this case, these elements must be proven to be part of the crime for the defendant to be found guilty. In order for the entire crime to be proven, all of the elements (or parts) of that crime must be proven first.

Mens Rea: Intent

One of the most important parts of criminal law is the prosecution's proof of **mens rea**, which stands for the element of intent. In

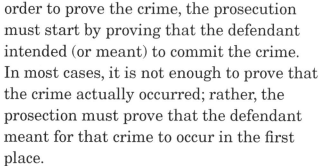

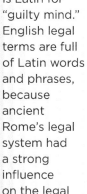

Mens rea is Latin for "guilty mind." English legal terms are full of Latin words and phrases, because ancient Rome's legal system had a strong influence on the legal systems of most Western countries.

order to prove the crime, the prosecution must start by proving that the defendant intended (or meant) to commit the crime. In most cases, it is not enough to prove that the crime actually occurred; rather, the prosecution must prove that the defendant meant for that crime to occur in the first place.

Under common law, to prove mens rea the prosecutor has to prove the following:

- The defendant acted *intentionally*, meaning that the defendant meant to commit the crime and cause the harm that resulted.

- The defendant acted *knowingly*, meaning that he or she knew or should have known that he was committing the crime and that harm could result.

- The defendant acted *recklessly*, meaning that he or she was aware of the potential adverse consequences of his or her actions, but disregarded them and committed those actions anyway.

- The defendant acted *negligently*, meaning that while he or she did not intentionally commit the crime, the defendant should have foreseen the potentially adverse consequences of his or her actions.

Each of these instances of mens rea can be proven, depending on the crime committed. For instance, a driver who drives while texting on his cell phone and then hits and kills a pedestrian may be found guilty of negligent homicide—even if the driver never intended to hurt anyone—because he acted recklessly. He was aware of the potential adverse consequences of his actions, but he disregarded them and committed those actions anyway. In another example, a mother who leaves her two-year-old toddler home alone to go to a bar and then comes home to find the child has been injured is guilty, because she should have foreseen the potentially adverse consequences of her actions.

Actus Reus: Action

The next important element that the prosecution must prove in any crime is **actus reus**, the act of committing the crime. In other words, the prosecution must prove that the defendant actually took part in the action that caused a crime to be committed. For example, in order to prove that the defendant is guilty of shoplifting, the prosecution must prove that the defendant actually took the items in question. If it cannot be proven that the defendant did so (perhaps because the defendant successfully argues that he intended to pay for the items), then the element of actus reus is missing.

In some instances, it is not necessary for the defendant to do anything particular in order to be guilty of a crime. In some cases, it is the failure to do something that counts! For instance, a parent who fails to save his or her child from death when the parent had the clear chance to save that child may be guilty of manslaughter, because the parent had a duty to act and failed to do so.

Each particular crime has its own specific elements that must be proven, in addition to mens rea and actus reus. You will learn about those specific elements in the next few chapters.

The Burden of Proof

You might have heard the saying that a criminal defendant is "innocent until proven guilty." In a criminal case, the **burden of proof** is on the prosecution. This means that the prosecution must prove every element of every crime charged. When it comes to defenses, the burden of proof is on the defendant. This means that the defendant must prove every element of every defense that he or she brings.

The Standard of Proof

In a criminal case, the standard of proof is "beyond a **reasonable doubt**." This means that no logical explanation can be derived from the facts of the case other than that the defendant committed the crime. For example, if a jury has no doubt that the defendant committed the crime because the entire crime by the defendant was caught on video and the defendant has offered no explanation, then the jury might find the defendant guilty beyond a reasonable doubt. However, if the defendant successfully offers a defense or alibi, then the jury might have reasonable doubt about the defendant's guilt.

Felonies and Misdemeanors

Certain types of crimes are considered more serious than others, which means they will carry more serious and significant punishments. Those crimes are called **felonies**. Other crimes are considered less serious; they are called **misdemeanors**. Note that which crimes are felonies and which are misdemeanors depend on the jurisdiction—so, a crime could be a felony in one state but only a misdemeanor in another.

Discussion Questions

1. Think of some examples where the case does NOT meet the reasonable doubt standard.

2. Have you ever observed a criminal trial, whether in real life or on the news? Was the defendant found guilty? What did the prosecution have to prove in that case?

Writing Prompts

1. You represent the prosecution in a murder case. Write a checklist of items that you will have to prove at trial.

_____

_____

_____

_____

2. Now, switch sides. As the defense attorney, how will your checklist differ?

_____

_____

_____

_____

TEST

Multiple Choice Questions:

Circle the correct answer.

1. Which of the following is a purpose for having criminal laws in place?

   A. Deterrence
   B. Reform

   C. Punishment
   D. All of the above

2. What is the legal term for the element of intent?

   A. Mens rea
   B. Actus reus

   C. Precedent
   D. Deterrence

3. Which of the following can be used by the prosecution to prove intent?

   A. The defendant acted intentionally.
   B. The defendant acted knowingly.
   C. The defendant acted recklessly.
   D. All of the above

4. "Beyond a reasonable doubt" refers to:

   A. The burden of proof
   B. The standard of proof
   C. Mens rea
   D. Actus reus

5. What is the term for providing the defendant with the opportunity to make good?

   A. Rehabilitation
   B. Punishment
   C. Deterrence
   D. Redress

6. What must the prosecution prove in a criminal case?

   A. Mens rea
   B. Actus reus
   C. Elements of the crime
   D. All of the above

7. If a defendant meant to steal someone's wallet, the defendant would most likely be acting how?

   A. Intentionally
   B. Knowingly
   C. Recklessly
   D. Negligently

8. Which of the following is NOT an example of a criminal law?

   A. A law that sets forth the elements of a crime
   B. A law that provides for criminal defenses
   C. A law that encourages crime in all states
   D. A law that provides for penalties for criminal conduct

9. Which of the following is NOT a potential job of the criminal defense attorney?

   A. To disprove the prosecution's case
   B. To convict the defendant
   C. To show that the defendant did not commit the crime
   D. To prove a valid defense to the crime

10. From where do criminal laws originate?

   A. Federal statutes
   B. State statutes
   C. Cases
   D. All of the above

True or False Questions:

Circle the correct answer.

1. Past cases make no difference during a case that is currently in court. T F

2. The burden of proof is on the prosecution during a criminal case. T F

3. All murder crimes are considered federal offenses. T F

4. Felonies typically carry more serious punishments than misdemeanors. T F

5. In some instances, the element of intent may be proven even if the defendant did not mean to cause any harm with his or her actions. T F

6. In some cases, actus reus can be proven by the failure to act. T F

7. Under the U.S. Constitution, criminally accused persons have the right to their day in court. T F

8. The role of the prosecutor is to defend the criminal defendant. T F

9. All criminal cases have past precedent on which the court can rely. T F

10. Criminal law protects the community and victims, and the accused. T F

Short Answer Questions:

1. Explain the various purposes and goals of criminal law.

_____

_____

_____

_____

_____

2. Discuss the roles of a prosecutor during a criminal trial.

_____

_____

_____

_____

_____

3. Discuss the roles of a defense attorney during a criminal trial.

_____

_____

_____

_____

_____

Chapter 3

CRIMES AGAINST THE PERSON

- Battery
- Assault
- Robbery
- Kidnapping
- Murder and Manslaughter

Some crimes are committed by one person against another person. These are serious offenses, and many of them carry very tough penalties or punishments.

Battery

A **battery** occurs when the defendant intentionally uses force on the body of another person. A slap, a punch, or a hit are all examples of battery. A battery can occur by use of an object. For example, hitting someone with a baseball bat— or intentionally throwing a baseball at someone—can be a battery.

Assault

An **assault** is committed when the defendant intentionally puts the victim in apprehension (fear) of an immediate physical attack. In other words, an assault occurs when physical battery is threatened. An example of an assault is raising a fist and pretending to punch the victim. Another example is throwing a bottle toward the victim. Even if the victim is not hit and no physical battery occurs, an assault is complete because there was an immediate threat.

Robbery

A **robbery** occurs when the defendant steals something from the victim's body by using force or the threat of force. When a defendant sticks a gun at a victim and demands that the victim hand over his or her wallet, a robbery occurs.

Kidnapping

A **kidnapping** takes place when the defendant takes the victim and brings him or her someplace else against the victim's will. Kidnapping can happen by force (such as by physically dragging a person into a car and driving off) or by threats or lures (such as by bribing a small child with the promise of candy and then taking the child away).

Murder and Manslaughter

The most significant and serious crime against the person is called **homicide**, which means killing of another human being. **Murder** is the killing of another human being with malice aforethought. **Malice aforethought** indicates **premeditation**, meaning the defendant thought about and planned the killing before actually committing it.

Malice can be proven in the following ways:

- **The defendant had the intent to kill the victim**.

  Example: The defendant puts poison into his boss's lunch, hoping the boss will die and the defendant will be promoted to the boss's job. The boss dies. The defendant is guilty of murder.

- **The defendant had the intent to seriously injure the victim**.

  Example: The defendant is playing baseball when he sees someone he does not like walking by. The defendant whips the baseball at the victim's head, intending to hit him but not necessarily kill him. The victim suffers a brain injury and dies as a result. The defendant is guilty of murder.

- **The defendant had reckless disregard for human life**.

   Example: The defendant shoots into a crowded house where he knows there is a party going on. One victim is shot in the chest and dies. The defendant is guilty of murder.

- **The defendant killed the victim during the commission of a dangerous felony**.

   Example: The defendant robs a bank while holding a gun. The gun goes off and kills the bank teller. The defendant is guilty of murder.

Manslaughter is another form of homicide, which is generally considered a less serious offense and carries less serious penalties than murder. Manslaughter can be voluntary or involuntary.

Voluntary manslaughter is the intentional killing of another human being with provocation (pressure or teasing), or killing in the "heat of passion." Voluntary manslaughter occurs when the defendant means to kill the victim, but does so after being provoked—for example, during a fight. In order for the charges to be reduced from murder to voluntary manslaughter, the defendant must not have had adequate time to "cool down" from being provoked. In other words, if the defendant has time to think about killing the victim, then that killing is not in the "heat of the moment" and will therefore be considered murder rather than manslaughter.

Involuntary manslaughter is the unintentional killing of another human being. Involuntary manslaughter takes place where the defendant does not mean to kill (or maybe even hurt) the victim, but an accidental killing results nonetheless. For example, a person driving too fast who hits and kills a pedestrian might be guilty of involuntary manslaughter.

Certain types of killings are considered by the law to be "justifiable" killings, where the defendant might not be punished for a death that results from his or her actions. The most prevalent example is **self-defense**: If a burglar breaks into a home and threatens to kill the owner of the home, but the owner kills the burglar instead, then the owner likely will not be guilty of homicide, because he killed while defending his own life.

Discussion Questions

1. Is there justifiable murder in the following situations:
    a. Protecting one's child from a burglar during a home invasion?
    b. Protecting one's friend in a fight that was started by someone else?
    c. Protecting yourself during a fight that you started?
    d. Using a gun in a fight where the other person is unarmed?

2. How is assault different from battery?

3. Explain the difference between voluntary and involuntary manslaughter.

Writing Prompts

1. What do you think are appropriate penalties for murder? Why? Discuss your answer fully.

_____

_____

_____

_____

2. Why are crimes against persons considered some of the most serious offenses? Explain.

_____

_____

_____

_____

Chapter 4

CRIMES INVOLVING PROPERTY

- Larceny
- Burglary
- Arson
- Fraud
- Receiving Stolen Property
- Forgery

Some crimes involve not the victim's person, but rather the victim's property. Many of these crimes also carry significant punishment.

Larceny

Larceny is the taking and carrying away of the property of another person, with the intent to permanently deprive the person of that property. Shoplifting is one form of larceny. Stealing a car is another. Stealing something from another person, in most

The word *petit* (from French meaning "small") can also be spelled *petty*, meaning "trivial or of little importance." Petit larceny is also referred to as petty theft.

cases, will constitute larceny.

Some states make a distinction between *grand larceny*, which is used when the property is worth over a certain amount of money, and *petit larceny*, if the property is worth under that amount.

Burglary

Burglary is committed when the defendant breaks and enters into another person's dwelling (home) at night with the intent to steal or to commit some other felony. For example, if a defendant enters his neighbor's home during the night without permission in order to take the neighbor's lawn mower, then the defendant has committed burglary. Under modern rules, the burglary definition has been expanded to apply to daytime as well as night; it has also been expanded to apply to many different types of buildings, such as businesses.

Arson

Arson is committed when the defendant intentionally and maliciously burns down a building. In the old days, only dwellings (one's home) counted for purposes of arson. Today, however, other buildings (such as businesses) also count.

Fraud

Fraud is wrongful or intentional deception, in which the defendant engages for some financial or personal gain. For instance, if the defendant steals the victim's personal information in order to apply for a credit card and then goes on a shopping spree, that constitutes fraud.

Receiving Stolen Property

This crime is committed when the defendant knowingly receives stolen property from another person. For example, when a garage mechanic receives a stolen car from the car thief, in order to strip the car down and sell it for its parts. Even though the mechanic did not steal the property, he or she can still be guilty of this crime if he or she received the stolen goods.

Forgery

Forgery involves the wrongful or intentional forging (copying or faking) of a document. For example, if a defendant writes a check to himself from the victim's checking account and deposits it in his own account, then he has committed forgery, in addition to the theft of the victim's money.

Discussion Questions

1. Explain what larceny is by listing five examples of it.

2. In some cases, a defendant can be held responsible for a property crime even if he or she was not the person who actually stole the property (for example, in the case of receiving stolen property). Is this fair? Why or why not?

Writing Prompts

1. Describe a situation where you observed someone's property being damaged or stolen (whether from your own experiences, through talking with others, reading about it, or seeing it on television). What happened to the person responsible? What happened to the property? Was the outcome what you hoped for?

_____

_____

_____

_____

2. In some cases, the criminal laws regarding property have been extended over time. For example, while arson and burglary used to apply only to "dwellings," those crimes now also apply to other buildings, such as businesses. Why was this process of extending liability necessary? Discuss your answer fully.

_____

_____

_____

_____

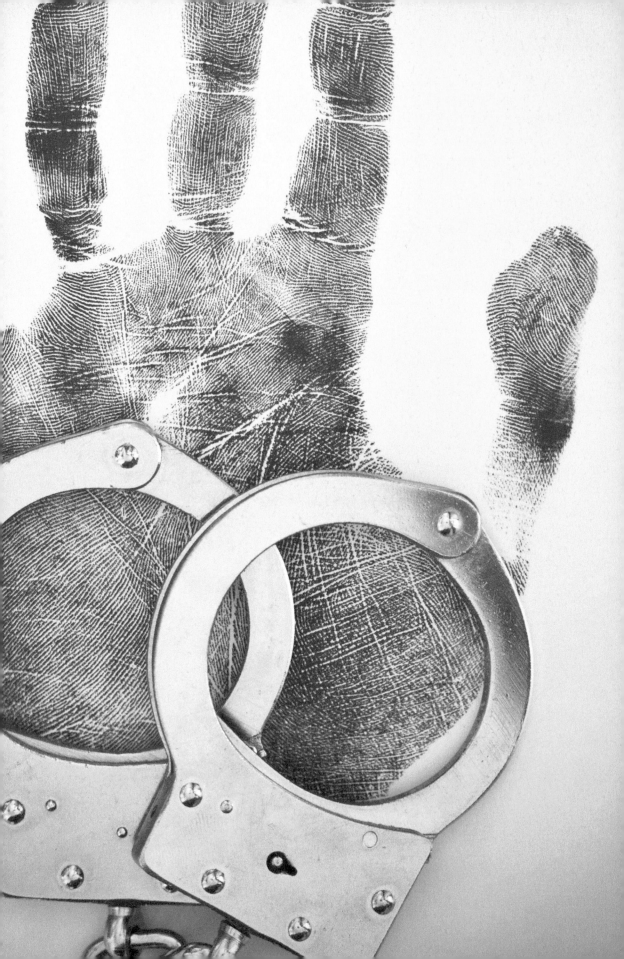

Chapter 5

OTHER CRIMES

- Crimes Against Society
- Conspiracy
- Attempt
- Solicitation
- Accomplice Liability

So far, you have learned about various crimes against the person and crimes involving property. This chapter discusses some other types of crimes.

Crimes Against Society

According to the website of the Federal Bureau of Investigation (www.fbi.gov), crimes against society "represent society's prohibition against engaging in certain types of activity; they are typically victimless crimes in which property is not the object." Examples include gambling where it is illegal, drug possession (ownership) and the selling of drugs, weapon law violations, disorderly conduct, driving under the influence of alcohol or drugs, and curfew and loitering violations.

Conspiracy

Have you ever "conspired" with a friend to play a prank on someone, or to convince your parents to let you stay up late? In criminal cases, conspiracy is considered a crime in and of itself. **Conspiracy** occurs when two or more people agree to commit a crime— for example, when two defendants agree to rob a bank together. Even if the robbery never takes place, the two defendants have already agreed to commit a crime together, which means they can be held guilty of the separate crime of conspiracy.

Each co-conspirator (a person who engages in the conspiracy) can be held **liable** (responsible) for the full extent of whatever occurs during the conspiracy. If, for example, the bank robbery goes wrong and a bank teller is killed as a result of a gunshot fired by one co-conspirator, then both co-conspirators can be held guilty of the bank teller's murder.

Attempt

In some cases, a defendant does not have to be successful at committing the crime in order to be held criminally liable. The crime of **attempt** covers inchoate, or incomplete, crimes. It occurs where a defendant tries to

commit a crime, plans for that crime, and takes a substantial step toward completing that crime. For example, if the defendant goes to buy a gun, goes to the victim's home, and shoots at the victim through the window, then the defendant will be guilty of attempted murder.

An attempt charge and a charge for the actual crime are not brought at the same time against the same defendant. After all, if the defendant succeeds in completing the crime, then that is no longer just an attempt, but rather the actual completed crime! For example, if in the previous scenario the defendant actually succeeds in killing the victim, then the defendant is charged with murder, not attempted murder.

Solicitation

Solicitation occurs where a defendant asks someone else to commit a crime. For example, if the defendant asks his friend to come with him to rob a bank, then the defendant is guilty of solicitation—even if the friend says no, and the bank robbery never occurs.

Accomplice Liability

An **accomplice** is a person who participates in a crime in some way but does not take part in the same exact crime as the **principal** (the person who actually commits the crime).

As an example, a person may be charged with being an accomplice if he helps a bank robber get away from the scene of the robbery, or if he hides the robber in his house while the police are looking for the criminal.

Discussion Questions

1. Why is it important to punish crimes against society, even if there are no victims and no property is involved?

2. How can attempt be proven?

3. Is it fair to hold a co-conspirator liable for all actions that the other co-conspirators committed? Why or why not?

Writing Prompt

1. What, in your opinion, are the most serious and detrimental crimes affecting society today? Discuss your answer fully.

_____

_____

_____

_____

Chapter 6

DEFENSES TO CRIMES

- Insanity
- Self-Defense and Defense of Others
- Defense of Property and Dwelling
- Other Defenses

As you must know, there are at least two sides to every story. In a criminal case, the defendant has the right to tell his or her side. One of the most significant parts of the defendant's case is the ability to present defenses.

Insanity

Have you ever heard the term that someone is "pleading insanity"? This refers to a defense to criminal liability for certain persons who can prove that they did not know right from wrong when they committed their crimes.

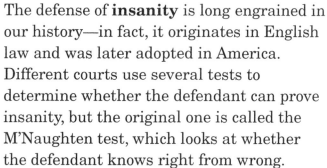

The defense of **insanity** is long engrained in our history—in fact, it originates in English law and was later adopted in America. Different courts use several tests to determine whether the defendant can prove insanity, but the original one is called the M'Naughten test, which looks at whether the defendant knows right from wrong.

Webster's Dictionary defines *insanity* as "the state of being seriously mentally ill; suffering from madness; extreme foolishness or irrationality."

The effect of a successful insanity defense depends on the jurisdiction. In some states, the defendant is found guilty but not sent to prison, but rather sent to a treatment center. In other states, the defendant's insanity plea can result in an acquittal.

Self-Defense and Defense of Others

Under some circumstances, criminal conduct can be justifiable by the defense of self-defense. For example, consider a situation where a robber holds a victim at gunpoint, and the victim takes out her own gun and shoots and kills the robber. The victim has technically committed murder, but she may use the defense of self-defense to escape criminal liability. The force used during self-defense must be reasonable—that is, it cannot seriously exceed the force posed by the dangers at hand.

Likewise, there is a defense called defense of others. For example, a parent may use this defense when protecting her children from the same robber.

Defense of Property and Dwelling

In some cases, a homeowner is allowed to defend his or her own property by use of force against an intruder, even if no person is being defended—for example, when no one is home. Some jurisdictions do not allow the use of deadly force to defend property.

Other Defenses

The defendant's case does not just hinge upon his or her proving a defense. As discussed in Chapter 2, the defendant can also win the case if the prosecution *fails* to prove its case beyond a reasonable

doubt. For example, the defendant can argue that the prosecution failed to prove the element of intent; if the jury agrees with the defendant, then the defendant will be acquitted (cleared of charges). The defendant can also challenge the case by offering pertinent facts—for instance, that the defendant had an alibi at the time the crime was committed.

State v. Larry: The Facts

Let's look at the fictitious case of *State v. Larry*. MyFace is a social network with millions of members internationally. It is popular in particular with secondary school students and college students. Anytown High School (AHS) is a public school in Anytown, State, which serves students in grades 9 through 12. Anytown Community College (ACC) is a public two-year junior college in Anytown.

Larry, an 18-year-old student at AHS, has set up a "community page" on MyFace titled "The AHS Vampire Lovers Club," an extracurricular organization at AHS of which Larry is president. The club (consisting of about a dozen active students) meets a few times per week at AHS at lunch to discuss vampires in the context of popular culture. The purpose of the community page is to further allow students to discuss vampires off-campus, but the page is open and visible to the public.

One month ago, AHS held an impromptu

back-to-school assembly at lunch, at which every student's attendance was mandatory. As a result of the assembly, the club's members were unable to hold their usual meeting. Hank, a high school student at AHS and a member of the Vampire Lovers Club, posted a message on the community page titled "Principal Smitty is a Major Tool," whereby Hank discussed the various shortcomings of the AHS principal, including that: "Smitters is so stupid that he can't even spell AHS, we don't want or need another stupid assembly and should have had the right to have the meeting we really wanted to go to!! But then again stupid Smitty does not care about his students and only cares about his paycheck!! Someone needs to blow Smitty to smithereens!!!"

The following day, Principal Smitty called Hank into his office and demanded that Hank delete his posting and any comments on it from the club's MyFace page. The same day, Principal Smitty sent Hank's parents a letter, stating that effective immediately, he has suspended Hank for two weeks and forbade Hank from participating in any extracurricular activities for the remainder of the school year.

Principal Smitty wrote to MyFace, informing the network that the Vampire Lovers Club was no longer welcome at the school, and requesting that MyFace remove the community page. Principal Smitty also indicated that the page included at least one posting that defamed Principal Smitty's character. He threatened to take legal action if MyFace did not take down the page. In accordance with its user policy, MyFace removed the postings by Hank and Anonymous, but left the community page otherwise untouched.

A week later, Larry drove to AHS brandishing a baseball bat, and he battered Principal Smitty, who suffered serious injuries as a result.

Discussion Questions

1. What is permissible as "reasonable force" during self-defense? For example, is it permissible to use a gun where the aggressor (the person who attacks) does not have a gun? Can you think of other circumstances where the use of force becomes an issue?

2. Is it fair to have an insanity defense in place? Why or why not?

Writing Prompt

1. What does it mean to allow the defendant to tell his or her story in court? Discuss your answer fully.

_____

_____

_____

_____

TEST

Multiple Choice Questions:

Circle the correct answer.

1. Which is a crime against society?

   A. Murder
   B. Battery

   C. Burglary
   D. Drug possession

2. What crime involves the agreement by two or more persons to commit a crime?

   A. Conspiracy
   B. Attempt

   C. Battery
   D. Assault

3. What crime involves the malicious burning of a building?

   A. Attempt
   B. Assault

   C. Arson
   D. Fraud

4. Which of the following is most likely to be the charge for a defendant who tries to steal a victim's wallet but does not succeed?

   A. Conspiracy
   B. Assault

   C. Attempt
   D. Shoplifting

5. If you were defending your mother against an attack and killed the intruder, which criminal defense would you present in court?

   A. Self-defense
   B. Defense of others
   C. Insanity
   D. None of the above

6. What crime is committed when the defendant shoots a person who has made him angry by provoking the defendant?

A. Murder
B. Involuntary manslaughter
C. Voluntary manslaughter
D. No crime

7. What crime is committed when the defendant accidentally kills a pedestrian while driving negligently?

A. Murder
B. Voluntary manslaughter
C. Involuntary manslaughter
D. No crime

8. Which of the following crimes is committed when the defendant tries to kill a person but does not succeed?

A. Battery
B. Murder
C. Manslaughter
D. Attempt

9. What is the term for asking someone else to commit a crime?

A. Conspiracy
B. Attempt
C. Solicitation
D. Robbery

10. Which of these is an example of a battery?

A. Punching the victim
B. Hitting the victim with a car, intentionally
C. Slamming the victim with a baseball bat
D. All of the above

True or False Questions:

Circle the correct answer.

1. Murder is the most serious crime against a person. T   F

2. No killing can ever be considered justifiable. T   F

3. Involuntary manslaughter is the unintentional killing of another human being. T   F

4. Assault and battery are the same crime. T   F

5. Today, only homes can be the object of arson. T   F

6. In order to claim an insanity defense, a person must be currently institutionalized. T   F

7. Burglary requires that the defendant break into and enter a building with the intent to steal or commit a felony. T   F

8. Each co-conspirator can be held liable for the full extent of the crimes committed during the conspiracy. T   F

9. The charges of attempt to murder and murder of the same victim can be brought against a defendant at the same time. T   F

10. Voluntary manslaughter requires that the killing take place in the heat of passion with adequate provocation. T   F

Short Answer Questions:

1. Define *murder*, and then define *manslaughter*.

_____

_____

_____

_____

_____

2. Explain what *crimes against society* are, and give examples.

_____

_____

_____

_____

_____

3. List three *inchoate* (incomplete) crimes.

_____

_____

_____

_____

_____

Chapter 7

ARRESTS AND THE PRIVILEGE AGAINST SELF-INCRIMINATION

- What Is an Arrest?
- The "Probable Cause" Standard
- The "Reasonable Suspicion" Standard and "Stop-and-Frisks"
- The Privilege Against Self-Incrimination
- *Miranda v. Arizona*

What Is an Arrest?

An arrest occurs when the police seize someone by legal authority and take that person into custody. Some courts look at whether the person reasonably thought that he or she was not free to leave to determine whether an arrest occurred.

The "Probable Cause" Standard

Have you ever heard someone argue that the police had "no probable cause" to arrest a person? How would you feel if the police could stop and arrest you without any valid reason? The probable cause standard is in place to ensure that does not happen. It means that the police must have valid reasons to arrest a person—for example, by believing in good faith that the person was committing a crime, had just committed a crime, or was about to commit a crime.

As an example, say that a police officer is on patrol and observes a teenager "tagging" or marking a public building with graffiti. Because this action constitutes a crime, the officer has probable cause to arrest the teenager.

Now say that the officer observes the same teen running away from the tagged building while holding a spray paint can, and then the officer observes fresh graffiti on the wall. Again, the officer might have probable cause to arrest the teen, as long as the officer reasonably believes the teen committed the crime.

However, say that the same officer sees the same teen simply walking down the street with a can of spray paint, with no fresh graffiti involved. In that case, the officer will not have probable cause to make an arrest, because there is no indication that the person committed a crime.

The "Reasonable Suspicion" Standard and "Stop-and-Frisks"

A police officer may stop a person in some cases even without probable cause—for example, where the officer has "reasonable suspicion" that the person is dangerous or has observed the person committing a traffic violation such as speeding. In fact, the officer may stop and "frisk," or pat down, the person for weapons, if the officer is concerned for safety.

The Privilege Against Self-Incrimination

The Fifth Amendment provides the "privilege against self-incrimination." This means that citizens cannot be forced to say or do anything that would incriminate them, which means putting them in a position that could subject them to be accused of a crime. Say, for example, that a police officer stops a citizen and asks a question regarding the citizen's involvement or knowledge about a recent burglary. The citizen can invoke his or her "right to remain silent" and does not have to answer the question.

Miranda v. Arizona

The landmark case of *Miranda v. Arizona* deals with the importance of informing a defendant of his or her rights at the time an arrest is made, and discusses the privilege against self-incrimination. In that case, the police arrested Ernesto Miranda at his home on March 13, 1963, and then took him to a room at the police station for questioning. The police never advised Mr. Miranda that he had a right to have an attorney present for questioning. Mr. Miranda signed a confession, in which he admitted to the crime with which he was charged. The confession form said it was made voluntarily. Mr. Miranda signed the paper, which included the words "with full knowledge of my legal rights, understanding any statement I make may be used against me." In court, however, Mr. Miranda objected to the introduction of his "voluntary" confession into evidence. He claimed that he did not understand his rights at the time of signing, and that his confession was not voluntary after all.

The Supreme Court ruled that under the Constitution, police must provide certain protections. When the police conduct "custodial interrogations" (questioning of suspects while being held by the police), they must advise people being questioned that they (1) have the right to remain silent and that (2) anything they say may be used against them in a court of law, and that (3) they have the right to an attorney during questioning, and (4) if they cannot afford an attorney and desire one, one will be appointed for them prior to questioning.

The mere fact that Mr. Miranda signed the confession stating he had knowledge of his legal rights is not enough. People cannot knowingly and intelligently waive their rights without being told of the right to remain silent, that anything said could be used against them, that they have the right to an attorney, and if they cannot afford one, an attorney would be appointed for them. Because Mr. Miranda was not specifically advised about these rights, he was not afforded his Fifth Amendment right to prevent compelled self-incrimination or his Sixth Amendment right to counsel. The U.S. Supreme Court reversed the Arizona Supreme Court's decision, in which Mr. Miranda was originally convicted of his crime, and he was let out of jail on parole in 1972. As a result of this case, these four rights are now known as the *Miranda* warning.

The *Miranda* Warning

- You have the right to remain silent.
- Anything you say can be used against you in a court of law.
- You have the right to an attorney.
- If you cannot afford an attorney, one will be appointed for you.

State v. Larry: The Arrest

Principal Smitty's secretary, Doris, called the Anytown Police Department right after the beating occurred. The APD sent out two cruisers. Larry was apprehended in the AHS parking lot by Officer Jones, an APD officer. Officer Jones yelled for Larry to stop, and when Larry began running, Officer Jones chased him on foot. Officer Jones was able to catch up with Larry and put him under arrest. Officer Jones then drove Larry to the Anytown police station. Officer Jones informed Larry of his *Miranda* rights: that he had a right to remain silent, that anything he said could be held against him in a court of law, that he had a right to an attorney, and that if he could not afford an attorney, one would be provided for him.

At the police station, Detective Smith came to question Larry about the beating. Larry refused to answer any questions. Detective

Smith continued to question Larry for an hour. Larry then asked to speak with an attorney. Detective Smith continued asking Larry questions for another 20 minutes, at which point Larry, who was exhausted and scared, blurted out: "I beat the stupid guy, okay? Now stop asking me stuff!"

Discussion Questions

1. List three circumstances that are enough to give rise to probable cause.

2. Explain the differences between probable cause to arrest and reasonable suspicion to stop and frisk.

Writing Prompts

1. Why is it essential to have constitutional protections such as the privilege against self-incrimination?

_____

_____

_____

_____

2. Research how *Miranda* has been followed in your state and discuss here.

_____

_____

_____

_____

Chapter 8

SEARCHES

- What is a Search?
- The "Reasonable Expectation of Privacy" Standard
- Search Warrant Requirements
- Valid Warrantless Searches
- The Exclusionary Rule
- The "Fruit of the Poisonous Tree" Standard

What Is a Search?

The Fourth Amendment protects against "unreasonable searches and seizures." This means that the police cannot stop citizens without a valid reason to do so, nor can they search citizens and their belongings without a valid reason.

In the context of law enforcement, a *seizure* means "the action of confiscating or impounding property by warrant of legal right."

The "Reasonable Expectation of Privacy" Standard

In order for a search to be in effect, the person searched must have a "reasonable expectation of privacy." For example, a person can expect that his or her home will be kept largely private; however, a person cannot expect to remain private if he or she does something illegal in a public place.

Search Warrant Requirements

In order to search a person or his or her house or belongings, police must have a valid search warrant. A **search warrant** is a document, issued by a judge or court, that (1) notes the reasons for conducting a search, (2) describes the proper ways in which the search must be conducted, and (3) gives the police authority to perform the search.

Valid Warrantless Searches

There are also many valid reasons for conducting a warrantless search, for which no search warrant will be required. Some examples include the following:

- Where the police see "in plain view" that a person is doing something illegal, such as selling drugs
- Where the police believe that there exists an emergency, such as when they are chasing a suspect in "hot pursuit"

- Where the police tow an automobile and want to perform an "inventory" search of the car

- Where the police believe that a suspect will try to destroy evidence within the time the police might spend in trying to get a warrant, such as a situation where a drug dealer will flush drugs down the toilet

- At the borders of countries and at airports, where national security issues are highly important

- Where the police lawfully arrest a suspect for committing a crime and search the suspect's clothing and belongings

- Where the person being searched gives permission ("consent") to the search

The Exclusionary Rule

The exclusionary rule states that evidence that is obtained by the police illegally will not be admissible at trial. In other words, if the police take some evidence from the defendant without having proper legal reasons for taking it, then the court in the ensuing criminal case against the defendant will not allow the jury to even consider the evidence.

For example, say that a police officer illegally searches a suspect's car without a valid warrant or any valid reasons for a warrantless search, and say that the officer finds an unregistered gun in the car's glove box. If the suspect is tried in court for a weapons offense, the gun will likely be excluded from evidence, and the jury will not get to consider it.

The "Fruit of the Poisonous Tree" Standard

Along the same lines, the "fruit of the poisonous tree" doctrine holds that any evidence that stems from the illegally obtained evidence will also be excluded at trial. For example, if the suspect in the previous situation confesses to having a gun illegally after the officer seizes the gun, the confession will also be excluded, because it stemmed from the unlawful search of the car.

State v. Larry: The Search

After arresting Larry in the AHS parking lot, Officer Jones patted Larry down for weapons but found none. He found the baseball bat with which Larry beat Principal Smitty on the other side of the parking lot, where Larry had dropped it after the attack, and Officer Jones seized the baseball bat as evidence.

Officer Jones then searched Larry's car, which was located at the far end of the parking lot as well. Officer Jones reasoned that Larry's car was searched as a result of his valid arrest of Larry. Officer Jones found no further weapons or evidence of the battery. He did, however, seize Larry's cell phone and took that into evidence as well.

Discussion Questions

1. What is a search? What are some examples of searches?

2. What standard applies to searches?

3. List five examples of warrantless searches.

Writing Prompts

1. Explain the Fourth Amendment's protections against unreasonable searches and seizures.

_____

_____

_____

_____

2. You are the police officer in charge of a murder case, and you need to search the suspect's home. What will your search warrant need to include? Research your jurisdiction's requirements and discuss them here.

_____

_____

_____

_____

Chapter 9

THE RIGHT TO COUNSEL

- What Does the Right to Counsel Mean?
- When Does the Right to Counsel Apply?
- Examples Where There Is No Right to Counsel
- *Gideon v. Wainwright*

What Does the Right to Counsel Mean?

The Sixth Amendment of the U.S. Constitution provides accused persons with the right to counsel. The **right to counsel** means that the accused can be represented by an attorney at all "critical stages" during the prosecution. In fact, if the defendant cannot afford an attorney, one will be provided to the defendant free of charge. Attorneys called **public defenders** (or legal aid attorneys) represent people who need legal services but cannot afford to pay for them.

When Does the Right to Counsel Apply?

Note that the right to counsel applies only at "critical stages" in the case. This includes the trial itself, where the criminal defendant will have the right to have an attorney represent him or her. It also includes some other pretrial motion hearings, as well as the arraignment (charging) and indictment (formal accusation) stages, among others.

Examples Where There Is No Right to Counsel

During some parts of the criminal process, the criminal defendant does not have the automatic right to counsel. For example, there is no right to have an attorney present during the taking of fingerprints and DNA samples, nor at parole or probation hearings. However, some states may vary this rule and afford additional protections to its citizens.

Gideon v. Wainwright

The case of *Gideon v. Wainwright* provided an important protection to criminal defendants. In that case, Clarence Earl Gideon was accused of breaking and entering in Florida, on June 3, 1961, after a pool hall was burglarized and a witness claimed that he had seen Mr. Gideon leaving the pool hall with a wine bottle and money in his pockets. When Mr. Gideon's case was tried in court, he asked for the assistance of an attorney. He stated that he was too poor to afford an attorney, and he asked that one be provided for him.

The trial judge denied Mr. Gideon's request. He said that assistance of an attorney was only required in "capital" cases, or cases that could result in the death penalty. Because Mr. Gideon's case could only result in jail time, the judge ruled that he was not entitled to the assistance of an attorney.

Mr. Gideon was convicted of breaking and entering by the jury. He was sentenced to five years in jail. While in jail, Mr. Gideon appealed his case to the U.S. Supreme Court. He acted as his own attorney (a process called pro se representation), researched his own case, and wrote to the Court on prison stationery.

The Supreme Court sided with Mr. Gideon. The Court ruled that the assistance of counsel is a fundamental right and is essential for a fair trial. In essence, the Court said that no one—regardless of wealth or other factors—should have to face a criminal trial without the assistance of an attorney.

"[A]ny person haled into court, who is too poor to hire a lawyer, cannot be assured a fair trial unless counsel is provided for him," the Court noted. "This seems to us to be an obvious truth."

In the end, Mr. Gideon received a second, new trial, and he was acquitted of the crime.

State v. Larry: Meeting with the Attorney

Next, Larry meets with his attorney, Attorney Kyle, who was hired by Larry's parents. Attorney Kyle goes over the likely criminal charges that Larry might face in court, and explains what each charge means. He also asks Larry pertinent questions about Larry's version of the facts, along with any potential defenses that could be brought on Larry's behalf. Attorney Kyle discusses the potential punishments that Larry might face. Finally, he discusses the scope of his representation of Larry, along with his fees.

Discussion Questions

1. Why is the right to an attorney essential, particularly when it comes to criminal proceedings?

2. Why is the right to an attorney not absolute? Why would it be impractical to allow criminal defendants to have attorneys at every possible stage at trial?

3. Why is it important to provide free legal representation to people who cannot pay for an attorney's time?

Writing Prompt

1. Explain the Fourth Amendment's protections against unreasonable searches and seizures.

_____

_____

_____

TEST

Multiple Choice Questions:

Circle the correct answer.

1. Which of the following is defined as a governmental intrusion into a person, paper, or effects?

   A. Seizure   C. Counsel

   B. Search   D. *Miranda*

2. Which of the following is NOT a valid warrantless search?

   A. Where the police see "in plain view" that a person is doing something illegal, such as selling drugs

   B. Where the police believe that there exists an emergency, such as when they are chasing a suspect in "hot pursuit"

   C. Where the police tow an automobile and want to perform an "inventory" search of the car

   D. Where the police believe that the person has done something wrong

3. Which of the following is the proper term for the person who is being searched giving permission to search?

   A. Consideration   C. Consent

   B. Counsel   D. *Miranda*

4. Which of the following is NOT one of the *Miranda* rights afforded to accused persons?

   A. The right to remain silent

   B. The right to an attorney

   C. The right to a private trial

   D. The right to have an attorney provided free of charge if the person cannot afford one

5. Which of the following did Gideon (the defendant in *Gideon v. Wainwright*) do as part of his appeal?

   A. He acted as his own attorney.
   B. He researched his own case.
   C. He wrote to the Supreme Court on prison stationery.
   D. All of the above

6. Which amendment to the U.S. Constitution protects against unreasonable searches and seizures?

   A. The Fourth Amendment
   B. The Fifth Amendment
   C. The Sixth Amendment
   D. The Eighth Amendment

7. Which amendment to the U.S. Constitution provides for the right to counsel?

   A. The Fourth Amendment
   B. The Fifth Amendment
   C. The Sixth Amendment
   D. The Eighth Amendment

8. Which case provided suspects with the right to remain silent?

   A. *Miranda v. Arizona*   C. Both of the above
   B. *Gideon v. Wainwright*   D. None of the above

9. Which of the following occurs when the government seizes a person and takes the person into custody?

   A. A search   C. Custodial interrogation
   B. An arrest   D. Prosecution

10. What standard applies to arrests?

   A. Reasonable suspicion   C. Reasonable cause
   B. Probable suspicion   D. Probable cause

True or False Questions:

Circle the correct answer.

1. A person can expect a right to privacy even if he or she does something illegal in a public place. T   F

2. The government may conduct a search on anyone whom the police believe to be guilty of a crime. T   F

3. Acting as your own attorney is allowed in court, and it is done through a process called pro se representation. T   F

4. The Fifth Amendment provides the "privilege against self-incrimination." T   F

5. A citizen must always answer every question that is asked by a police officer. T   F

6. In order for a search to be in effect, the person searched must have a "reasonable expectation of privacy." T   F

7. An accused person has the right to counsel in all parts of the proceedings at trial. T   F

8. If the defendant cannot afford an attorney, one will be provided to the defendant free of charge. T   F

9. The police can arrest a person if the police officer believes that person is committing a crime. T   F

10. The exclusionary rule states that evidence that is obtained by the police illegally will not be admissible at trial. T   F

Short Answer Questions:

1. List five criminal procedure protections afforded by the Bill of Rights.

_____

_____

_____

_____

_____

2. List five "warrantless search" exceptions in the area of searches and seizures.

_____

_____

_____

_____

_____

3. Explain the concept of *Miranda* rights.

_____

_____

_____

_____

_____

Chapter 10

BEGINNING A CRIMINAL CASE

- Arraignments
- Criminal Pleas
- Indictments
- How the Criminal Justice Process Works

Arraignments

Typically, the event that officially starts off the criminal prosecution is called an **arraignment**. The arraignment is where a criminal defendant is formally charged with a crime, or multiple crimes. During the arraignment, the prosecution officially calls the criminal defendant before the court and announces the charges against the defendant.

Criminal Pleas

At the arraignment, the defendant is asked to enter a **criminal plea**. The defendant may plead guilty, which means he admits to having committed the crime(s) charged, or not guilty, which means he denies committing the crime(s). In some jurisdictions, there are other pleas available as well.

Indictments

In some cases, the event that begins the criminal process is an indictment. An **indictment** is a formal accusation that starts a criminal case, and it is often presented by the grand jury, which is a collection of people from the community who are designated to inquire into alleged crimes and determine whether the evidence is sufficient to warrant a criminal trial.

Following is a short overview from the Victims of Crime website (http://www .victimsofcrime.org/help-for-crime-victims /get-help-bulletins-for-crime-victims/the -criminal-justice-system) describing the criminal justice system and the beginnings of a criminal prosecution.

How the Criminal Justice Process Works

Below is a basic outline of the sequence of events in the criminal justice process, beginning when the crime is reported or observed. The process may vary according to the jurisdiction, the seriousness of the crime (felony or misdemeanor), whether the accused is a juvenile or an adult, and other factors. Not every case will include all these steps, and not all cases directly follow this sequence. Many crimes are never prosecuted because they are not reported, because no suspects can be identified, or because the available evidence is not adequate for the prosecutor to build a case.

Entry into the System

- **Report:** Law enforcement officers receive the crime report from victims, witnesses, or other parties (or witness the crime themselves and make a report).

- **Investigation:** Law enforcement investigates the crime. Officers try to identify a suspect and find enough evidence to arrest the suspect they think may be responsible.

- **Arrest or Citation:** If they find a suspect and enough evidence, officers may arrest the suspect or issue a citation for the suspect to appear in court at a specific time. This decision depends on the nature of the crime and other factors. If officers do not find a suspect and enough evidence, the case remains open.

Prosecution and Pretrial

- **Charges:** The prosecutor considers the evidence assembled by the police and decides whether to file written charges (or a complaint) or release the accused without prosecution.

- **First Court Appearance:** If the prosecutor decides to file formal charges, the accused will appear in court to be

informed of the charges and of his or her rights. The judge decides whether there is enough evidence to hold the accused or release him or her. If the defendant does not have an attorney, the court may appoint one or begin the process of assigning a public defender to represent the defendant.

- **Bail or Bond:** At the first court appearance (or at any other point in the process—depending on the jurisdiction) the judge may decide to hold the accused in jail or release him or her on bail, bond, or on his or her "own recognizance" (OR). This means the defendant promises to return to court for any required proceedings and the judge does not impose bail because the defendant appears not to be a flight risk. To be released on bail, defendants have to hand over cash or other valuables (such as property deeds) to the court as security to guarantee that the defendant will appear at the trial. Defendants may pay bail with cash or bond (an amount put up by a bail bondsman who collects a nonrefundable fee from the defendant to pay the bail). The judge will also consider such factors as drug use, residence, employment, and family ties in deciding whether to hold or release the defendant.

- **Grand Jury or Preliminary Hearing:** In about one-half of the states, defendants have the right to have their cases heard by a grand jury, which means that a jury of citizens must hear the evidence presented by the prosecutor and decide whether there is enough evidence to indict the accused of the crime. If the grand jury decides there is enough evidence, the grand jury submits to the court an indictment, or written statement of the facts of the offense charged against the accused. In other cases, the accused may have to appear at a preliminary hearing in court, where the judge may hear evidence and the defendant is formally indicted or released.

- **Arraignment:** The defendant is brought before the judge to be informed of the charges and his or her rights. The defendant pleads guilty, not guilty, or no contest (accepts the penalty without admitting guilt). If the defendant pleads guilty or no contest, no trial is held, and offender is sentenced then or later. If the defendant pleads not guilty, a date is set for the trial. If a plea agreement is negotiated, no trial is held.

Adjudication (Trial Process)

- **Plea Agreements:** The majority of cases are resolved by plea agreements rather than trials. A plea agreement means that the defendant has agreed to plead guilty to one or more of the charges in exchange for one of the following: dismissal of one or more changes, a lesser degree of the charged offense, a recommendation for a lenient sentence, not recommending the maximum sentence, or making no recommendation. The law does not require prosecutors to inform victims about plea agreements or seek their approval.

- **Trial:** Trials are held before a judge (bench trial) or judge and jury (jury trial), depending on the seriousness of the crime and other factors. The prosecutor and defense attorney present evidence and question witnesses. The judge or jury finds the defendant guilty or not guilty on the original charges or lesser charges. Defendants found not guilty are usually released. If the verdict is guilty, the judge will set a date for sentencing.

Post-Trial

- **Sentencing**: Victims are allowed to prepare for the judge (and perhaps to read at the sentencing hearing) a victim impact statement that explains how the crime affected them. In deciding on a sentence, the judge has a range of choices, depending on the crime. These choices include restitution (paying the victim for costs related to the crime), fines (paid to the court), probation, jail or prison, or the death penalty. In some cases, the defendant appeals the case, seeking either a new trial or to overturn or change the sentence.

- **Probation or Parole:** A judge may suspend a jail or prison sentence and instead place the offender on probation, usually under supervision in the community. Offenders who have served part of their sentences in jail or prison may—under certain conditions—be released on parole, under the supervision of the corrections system or the court. Offenders who violate the conditions of their probation or parole can be sent to jail or prison.

State v. Larry: The Arraignment

The day after the incident at AHS, Larry was formally arraigned in court and charged with assault and battery with a dangerous weapon, along with cyber-bullying. The prosecutor in charge briefly considered charging Larry with attempted murder of Principal Smitty—after all, Larry had originally posted on social media about "blowing Smitty to smithereens." Fearing that the mens rea (intention) for attempted murder would not be proven, however, and taking into consideration Larry's youth and lack of prior charges or convictions, the prosecutor decided to pursue a lesser-included charge of assault and battery.

At his arraignment, Larry was represented by his counsel, Attorney Kyle. The State was represented by the prosecutor, Attorney Flora. Through his attorney, Larry pleaded not guilty to all of the charges.

Discussion Questions

1. You are a criminal defense attorney, and your client wants to plead *not guilty* to the crimes with which he was charged. Give some examples of how you will advise your client.

2. Now assume that your client wants to plead *guilty* to the crimes with which he was charged. Give some examples of how you will advise your client.

Writing Prompt

1. What is the difference between resolution by a trial and resolution by a plea agreement? What are the advantages and disadvantages of plea agreements?

_____

_____

_____

Chapter 11

THE RIGHT TO A FAIR TRIAL

- Speedy, Public Jury Trials
- Right to Cross-Examine Witnesses

Speedy, Public Jury Trials

The Sixth Amendment provides a criminal defendant with the right to a speedy and public trial. It also provides the defendant with the right to a jury trial; in fact, the defendant will receive a trial by jury unless he or she affirmatively waives that right.

Right to Cross-Examine Witnesses

In addition, the Sixth Amendment provides a criminal defendant with the right to confront (**cross-examine**) witnesses that the government calls against the defendant. This means that the defendant's attorney can question the prosecution's witnesses while they are testifying, which means they are answering questions under oath during the trial. It also means that the defendant's attorney can discredit (harm the reputation of) the witnesses, which means offering evidence as to why those witnesses should not be believed by the jury—whether because there is (1) an issue with their bias (such as being related to the victim, for example), or (2) an issue with their abilities to witness or recall the events in question (such as not remembering part of the events), or (3) an issue with their general credibility and reputation (such as the witness previously having been convicted of a crime).

Under the Sixth Amendment, the defendant's attorney can also call and question his or her own witnesses to testify at trial, such as a person who can help the defendant prove an alibi. The defense can offer its own evidence during the trial as well—for example, a copy of the plane ticket proving that the defendant was out of town during the time when the crime was committed.

State v. Larry: The Trial

Attorney Kyle began preparing for Larry's trial. First, he submitted questionnaires to the potential jurors, asking them about their background, any involvement with the criminal process, and relationships to law enforcement personnel, among many other questions.

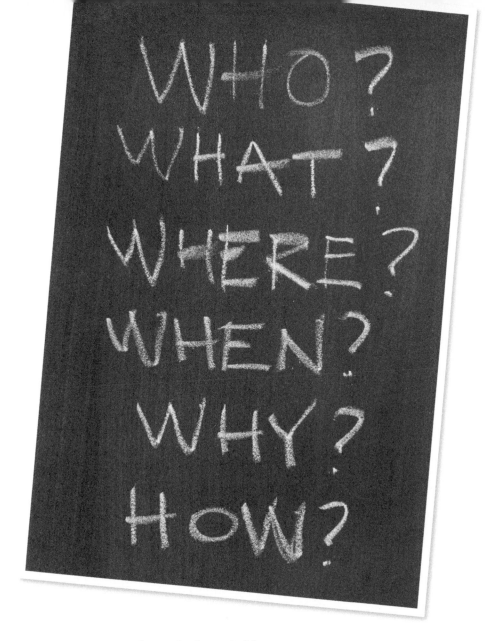

Once the jury was selected, the trial began. The prosecutor sought to introduce evidence taken from Larry's cell phone, along with the baseball bat, and Larry's statement at the police station. Attorney Kyle objected to all of those pieces of evidence. He argued that the evidence was obtained illegally and therefore must be excluded under the exclusionary rule and the "fruit of the poisonous tree" doctrine.

At trial, Attorney Kyle also introduced evidence that, at the time of the attack, Larry did not know right from wrong and therefore should not be held responsible for his actions. (The jurisdiction in which Larry lives allows for this as a potential defense). Both attorneys called witnesses. Larry considered testifying on his own behalf, but Attorney Kyle advised him not to, because he explained that Larry could evoke his privilege against self-incrimination under the Fifth Amendment and choose not to testify at trial.

The jury deliberated for just one hour before finding Larry guilty of all the charges. The jury did not believe Larry's defense. Fortunately for Larry, because this was his first conviction, the trial judge decided to be lenient. He sentenced Larry to community service and three years of probation only, with no jail time to be served. Larry was also ordered to pay a fine and pay retribution to the principal for his injuries and medical expenses.

Discussion Questions

1. What does it mean to have a "fair" trial? What are some of the considerations that go into "fairness?"

2. If you represented a criminal defendant, what types of jurors would you hope to have at your trial? What characteristics would you want them to have?

Writing Prompts

1. You represent a criminal defendant who is on trial for assault and battery of his neighbor. Write a questionnaire for the potential jurors.

_____

_____

_____

_____

2. You are the prosecutor in the above case for assault and battery. Write a checklist regarding how you will prepare for the trial.

_____

_____

_____

_____

Chapter 12

DOUBLE JEOPARDY AND CRUEL AND UNUSUAL PUNISHMENT

- The Protection Against Cruel and Unusual Punishment
- The Protection Against Double Jeopardy

The Protection Against Cruel and Unusual Punishment

The Eighth Amendment protects against cruel and unusual punishment. For example, a citizen who is found guilty of a crime cannot be beaten, or hit with sticks or canes, or tortured. Instead, that citizen is punished by some legal means, such as jail time, paying fines, or serving probation. In some cases of very serious crimes (such as killing another human being), some states may impose capital punishment, which means punishment by the death penalty.

The U.S. Supreme Court has addressed many situations where the protection against cruel and unusual punishment was

Capital Punishment

- The term **capital punishment** comes from the Latin *capitalis*, meaning "regarding the head," referring to the practice of beheading.
- The **death penalty** is a form of capital punishment, when someone is sentenced to death for a crime(s) he or she has been found guilty of committing.
- **Execution** is the act of carrying out the death penalty, by various means, including electrocution and lethal injection.

an issue. In a recent case, the Court said that juvenile defendants could not be given the death penalty. In another recent case, the Court said that mentally ill persons also could not be given the death penalty.

The Protection Against Double Jeopardy

The Eight Amendment also protects against "double jeopardy." This means that a person cannot be tried for the same crime twice, if that defendant has been acquitted of the crime or if he or she has served the sentence given after his or her conviction.

For example, say a criminal defendant has been tried for the murder of a victim and acquitted. The prosecution cannot then retry the defendant if it thinks of a better argument to use at trial. There are exceptions, depending on the jurisdiction, such as when significant new evidence comes to light about the case.

Discussion Questions

1. Is it a good idea that a criminal defendant cannot be tried twice for the same crime? Why or why not? What are some of the pros and cons of the double jeopardy standard?

2. In what ways has the idea of criminal punishment evolved over the years? Can you think of any additional examples of punishment that were used in previous times, which would now be considered cruel and unusual?

Writing Prompt

1. What are some examples that you believe constitute cruel and unusual punishment?

_____

_____

_____

_____

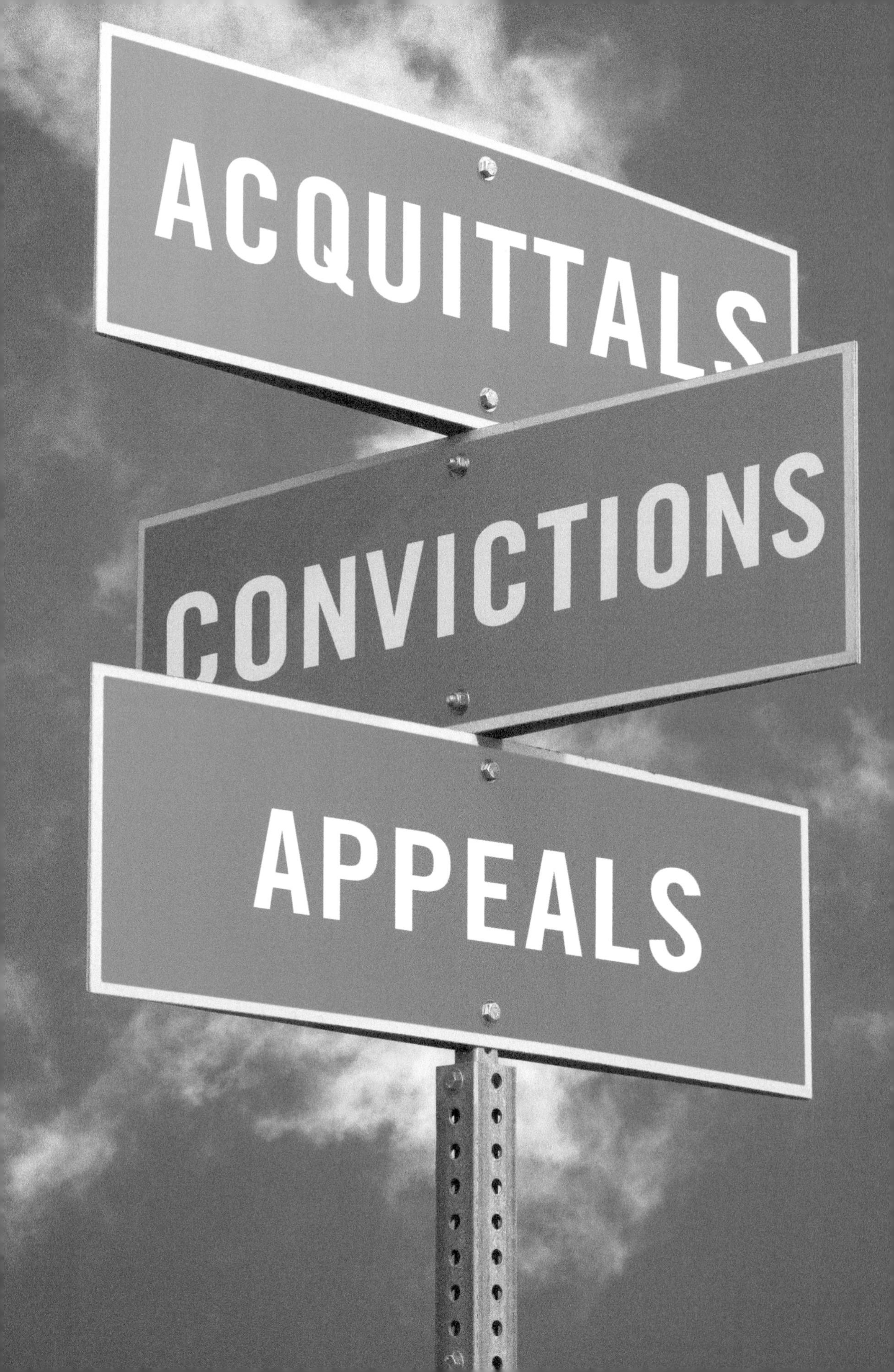
ACQUITTALS
CONVICTIONS
APPEALS

Chapter 13

ACQUITTALS, CONVICTIONS, AND APPEALS

- The Effect of an Acquittal
- The Effect of a Conviction
- Post-Conviction Motions
- The Basics of a Criminal Appeal

Once the jury takes the case for deliberation, a number of things can happen.

The Effect of an Acquittal

The defendant might be given an **acquittal**, which means that the jury has found the defendant not guilty of the crime(s) charged. In most cases, the defendant can then go free.

In some cases, the jury is unable to decide whether the defendant is guilty or not—while some jurors might find the defendant guilty, others disagree. In many states, this results in a mistrial, which might in turn result in a new trial to be held at a later time.

The Effect of a Conviction

The defendant might be given a **conviction**, which means the jury has found the defendant to be guilty. Once a conviction occurs, the next step is typically sentencing, which is the process by which punishment is given out. During sentencing, the judge will decide (1) whether the defendant should be given time in prison, and if so, for how long; (2) whether any fines must be paid by the defendant to the government or to the victim(s); and (3) whether any other penalties should be imposed—for example, ordering the defendant to perform community service.

Post-conviction Motions

After the trial, several motions might also be made. One example is a motion for a new trial, which requires the court to essentially scrap the judgment at trial and order a brand new fact-finding trial.

The Basics of a Criminal Appeal

If the defendant is found guilty, he or she might choose to appeal the case to a higher court. First, the defendant will file a notice of appeal in the court of appeals. Then, both parties will submit their appellate **briefs**, which are documents that contain the parties' positions on appeal. The parties then are invited for oral arguments, where they argue those positions to the court. In most cases, the parties argue in front of a panel (or selection) of judges; in rare cases, they are heard by the entire bench, meaning all of the appellate justices who work for the court.

The appellate court may *affirm* the trial court's judgment, which means the justices agree with it. It may instead *reverse* the trial court's judgment, which means the justices disagree with it. If the parties are still dissatisfied with the appellate court's judgment, they may further appeal the judgment to a state supreme court.

In very rare but important criminal cases, the case makes its way to the U.S. Supreme Court. In most cases, the prosecution may not appeal a criminal acquittal, unless some important procedural issue is at stake.

State v. Larry: Post-Trial

Larry discussed his post-trial options with Attorney Kyle, who explained that Larry could attempt to appeal his conviction based on the evidence that was introduced by the prosecution, to which Attorney Kyle had objected at the trial. However, Attorney Kyle explained that the appeal would be time-consuming and costly. After considering his options, Larry decided not to appeal. Instead, he focused on his future and on staying out of trouble!

Discussion Questions

1. What is the purpose of having a system for appealing a case in place?

2. In some cases, there are mandatory minimum and maximum sentences in place that must follow a conviction. For example, a judge must prescribe a sentence between one year and three years for a particular crime of which the defendant was convicted. Is this a good idea? Why or why not?

Writing Prompt

1. What are some examples of fair and reasonable sentences? What sentence should apply to murder, for example? To assault and battery? To an attempted crime? To burglary or theft crimes?

_____

_____

_____

_____

Multiple Choice Questions:

Circle the correct answer.

1. Which of the following refers to the proceeding that formally begins a criminal trial?

   A. Arraignment   C. Prosecution
   B. Indictment   D. None of the above

2. Which of the following refers to the proceeding whereby a grand jury can bring charges against a defendant?

   A. Arraignment   C. Prosecution
   B. Indictment   D. None of the above

3. Which amendment to the U.S. Constitution provides for the right to a jury trial in criminal cases?

   A. Fourth   C. Sixth
   B. Fifth   D. Eighth

4. Which amendment to the U.S. Constitution provides for the protection from double jeopardy?

   A. Fourth   C. Sixth
   B. Fifth   D. Eighth

5. What is the term for a jury who finds a defendant not guilty in a criminal case?

   A. Convict   C. Sentence
   B. Acquit   D. Appeal

6. Which of these does NOT take place after a criminal trial is over?

   A. Sentencing
   B. Appeal
   C. Motion for new trial
   D. Arraignment

7. What can an appeals court do with the trial court's judgment?

   A. Affirm
   B. Modify
   C. Reverse
   D. All of the above

8. Which of these rights does a defendant have?

   A. The right to a jury trial
   B. The right to a speedy trial
   C. The right to a fair trial
   D. All of the above

9. What is the term for questioning the other side's witnesses against you?

   A. Examsmanship
   B. Cross-examination
   C. Prosecution
   D. None of the above

10. During sentencing, the judge will decide:

   A. Whether the defendant should be given time in prison, and if so, for how long
   B. Whether any fines must be paid by the defendant to the government or to the victim(s)
   C. Whether any other penalties should be imposed
   D. All of the above

True or False Questions:

Circle the correct answer.

1. A criminal defendant can never be tried for more than one crime. T F

2. A criminal defendant cannot be tried for the same offense twice. T F

3. In the United States, criminal defendants are protected from cruel and unusual punishment. T F

4. A defendant cannot admit to committing a crime once he or she has been arrested. T F

5. The defendant's attorney can call and question his or her own witnesses to testify at trial. T F

6. If a defendant is found not guilty, he or she is typically allowed to go free. T F

7. In most cases, the prosecution may not appeal a criminal acquittal, unless some important procedural issue is at stake. T F

8. If a plea agreement is negotiated, no trial is held. T F

9. In some cases, the judge may order bail for the criminal defendant. T F

10. In some cases, the jury is unable to decide whether the defendant is guilty or not, which can result in a mistrial. T F

Short Answer Questions:

1. Explain the criminal trial process.

_____

_____

_____

_____

_____

2. Explain the appeals process.

_____

_____

_____

_____

_____

3. Explain what happens after a criminal defendant is found guilty.

_____

_____

_____

_____

_____

DEBATE #1:

Should cyber-bullying have the same consequences and punishments as bullying someone in real life?

1. Introduce your claim about this issue.

   Your claim:

   _____

   _____

   _____

2. Support your claim with logical reasoning and relevant, accurate data and evidence that demonstrate an understanding of the topic and rely on credible sources.

   Support:

   _____

   _____

   _____

   Support:

   _____

   _____

   _____

Support:

_____

_____

_____

3. Acknowledge alternate or opposing claims, and distinguish them from your claim by using well-thought-out, relevant counterclaims.

Alternate claim and counterclaim:

_____

_____

_____

Alternate claim and counterclaim:

_____

_____

_____

Alternate claim and counterclaim:

_____

_____

_____

4. Provide a conclusion that follows from and supports your claim presented.

In conclusion ...

Conclusion:

_____

_____

_____

DEBATE #2:

Should people who have been convicted of any crime (whether felony or misdemeanor) be allowed to hold political office?

1. Introduce your claim about this issue.

   Your claim:

   _____

   _____

   _____

2. Support your claim with logical reasoning and relevant, accurate data and evidence that demonstrate an understanding of the topic and rely on credible sources.

   Support:

   _____

   _____

   _____

   Support:

   _____

   _____

   _____

Support:

_____

_____

_____

3. Acknowledge alternate or opposing claims, and distinguish them from your claim by using well-thought-out, relevant counterclaims.

   Alternate claim and counterclaim:

   _____

   _____

   _____

   Alternate claim and counterclaim:

   _____

   _____

   _____

   Alternate claim and counterclaim:

   _____

   _____

   _____

4. Provide a conclusion that follows from and supports your claim presented.

   Conclusion:

   _____

   _____

   _____

In conclusion ...

DEBATE #3:

Should juvenile defendants be tried in the same court and face the same punishments as adult offenders?

1. Introduce your claim about this issue.

   Your claim:

   _____

   _____

   _____

2. Support your claim with logical reasoning and relevant, accurate data and evidence that demonstrate an understanding of the topic and rely on credible sources.

   Support:

   _____

   _____

   _____

   Support:

   _____

   _____

   _____

Support:

_____

_____

_____

3. Acknowledge alternate or opposing claims, and distinguish them from your claim by using well-thought-out, relevant counterclaims.

Alternate claim and counterclaim:

_____

_____

_____

Alternate claim and counterclaim:

_____

_____

_____

Alternate claim and counterclaim:

_____

_____

_____

4. Provide a conclusion that follows from and supports your claim presented.

Conclusion:

In conclusion ...

_____

_____

_____

DEBATE #4:

Some states have passed laws called "Three Strikes Laws," which require a judge to impose a life sentence (life in jail) on people who have committed three serious crimes. For example, in some states, a criminal who has been convicted of two burglaries and then is convicted of a third burglary can receive a life sentence. Do you believe that Three Strikes Laws should be legal?

I think...

1. Introduce your claim about this issue.

   Your claim:

   _____

   _____

   _____

2. Support your claim with logical reasoning and relevant, accurate data and evidence that demonstrate an understanding of the topic and rely on credible sources.

Support:

_____

_____

_____

Support:

_____

_____

_____

Support:

_____

_____

_____

3. Acknowledge alternate or opposing claims, and distinguish them from your claim by using well-thought-out, relevant counterclaims.

Alternate claim and counterclaim:

_____

_____

_____

Alternate claim and counterclaim:

_____

_____

_____

Alternate claim and counterclaim:

_____

_____

_____

4. Provide a conclusion that follows from and supports your claim presented.

Conclusion:

_____

_____

_____

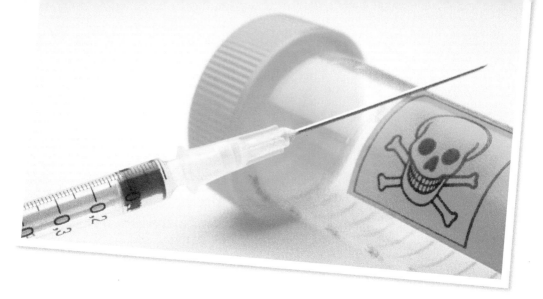

DEBATE #5:

Should the death penalty be abolished?

1. Introduce your claim about this issue.

   Your claim:

   _____

   _____

   _____

I think...

2. Support your claim with logical reasoning and relevant, accurate data and evidence that demonstrate an understanding of the topic and rely on credible sources.

   Support:

   _____

   _____

   _____

   Support:

   _____

   _____

   _____

Support:

_____

_____

_____

3. Acknowledge alternate or opposing claims, and distinguish them from your claim by using well-thought-out, relevant counterclaims.

Alternate claim and counterclaim:

_____

_____

_____

Alternate claim and counterclaim:

_____

_____

_____

Alternate claim and counterclaim:

_____

_____

_____

In conclusion ...

4. Provide a conclusion that follows from and supports your claim presented.

Conclusion:

_____

_____

_____

PART
2

CIVIL
TRIALS

Chapters 14–23

Chapter 14

COMMON TYPES OF CIVIL CASES

- Torts
- Contracts
- Property Disputes
- Business Disputes
- Family Disputes
- Civil Rights

Have you ever been in a disagreement? For example, have you ever had a fight with a sibling or a friend over who should play with a particular video game? Or, have you ever had a dispute with your parent over how late your curfew should be?

Civil cases involve private parties. The American court system sees—and helps resolve—many cases that deal with disagreements or disputes between private parties every year. **Litigation** is the process of resolving a civil case in court. Sometimes, when people have disputes or disagreements, it requires the involvement of the court system to settle them.

Torts

A **tort** is a private or civil wrong. Torts occur when someone (or a business) does something against another person, either intentionally or in the process of causing an accident. The court system allows parties who have been wronged to file a claim in court and to be compensated for the damages they suffered.

The party who is wronged, and therefore files a civil case, is called the **plaintiff**. The party who is allegedly responsible for the wrongdoing, and therefore must answer the civil case that was brought, is called the **defendant**. The plaintiff and defendant are called **parties** to the case.

Perhaps the most common tort is called **negligence**. Under negligence, a plaintiff may file a claim where the defendant is at fault for injuring the plaintiff. As an example, a negligence claim might involve a car accident. If a driver goes through a red light and hits a pedestrian, causing injuries, that pedestrian may sue the driver for negligence. Other negligence cases may involve personal injury matters, such as in the case of a plaintiff who slips and falls because of dangerous conditions. Still other negligence claims are brought against defendants who are professionals, such as doctors who fail to operate on a patient using the proper standard of care.

fail·ure
nonperformance of something due,
required, or expected

There is a defense to negligence called *comparative negligence*. This defense is brought when the plaintiff is partially or wholly responsible for the negligence that occurs. For example, in a car accident, the defendant may have failed to stop at a stop sign and caused a crash, but the plaintiff may have been speeding at the time of the accident. Therefore, the defendant can claim that the plaintiff was partially responsible for what happened. This is called comparative negligence.

Other torts focus on intentional conduct by a defendant. As an example, the tort of battery deals with intentional physical contact, such as slapping someone. The tort of assault involves intentional threats or putting someone in fear. And the tort of false imprisonment applies when the defendant holds someone in a confined space against his or her will.

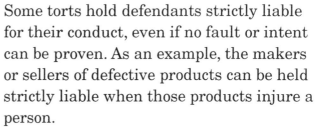

Some torts hold defendants strictly liable for their conduct, even if no fault or intent can be proven. As an example, the makers or sellers of defective products can be held strictly liable when those products injure a person.

A tort may be committed by a person, such as a driver who drives negligently and causes an accident. It may also be committed by a business entity, such as the maker of a product that becomes defective and dangerous and causes an injury to someone who uses that product.

Types of Torts

- Negligence
- Intentional Torts
- Strict Liability

Contracts

A **contract** is an agreement between two parties. It may be between individual persons or between entities such as businesses. Many contracts are used in everyday life; in fact, you might have copies of contracts in your own house! For example, your parents probably signed a contract for all of their utilities, such as cable, phone, or Internet service; for cellular phone service; and for their credit cards. According to those common contracts, one party (the service provider, such as the phone company) agrees to provide services, while the other party (the user, such as your parents) agrees to pay a specified amount for those services.

Other common contracts include purchase agreements, which are between a buyer and a seller. For example, if your parents own their own home, they may have signed a contract called a purchase and sales agreement when they bought it. (If your parents rent their home, they may have signed a lease, which is also a form of contract.) A buyer of a car also signs a contract with the dealer regarding the purchase price and other terms of ownership.

According to the law of contracts, if one of the parties to the contract fails to perform according to the terms of the contract, then the other party may sue in court. This court claim is called a *breach of contract* claim. The party who is wronged (also the plaintiff) may recover the money he or she lost when the other party (the defendant) breached the contract.

Property Disputes

Some court cases center around property. For example, a party may sue if the sale of a house goes wrong, such as where the buyer refuses to buy a house that he or she has signed a contract to buy previously. A landlord may sue his or her tenants for rent that is not paid, or for damaging the rental property.

Personal items can also be the basis for a lawsuit. For example, the tort of *conversion* applies when a defendant takes someone else's personal property, such as by taking a car for a "joyride" (a fast, often dangerous ride taken in a stolen car).

Business Disputes

Court cases are not limited to individual persons. In some cases, businesses engage in civil litigation. For example, a business may sue to have its **copyrights** (exclusive legal rights), trademarks, or trade secrets protected from others, such as in the case of a music company whose works are being "pirated" (downloaded illegally) or circulated on the Internet.

A business may also sue a former employee who is now competing against the business, provided that the employee previously signed a contract agreeing not to compete with the business for customers. Conversely, many cases deal with employment law, where an employee may sue a present or former employer. As an example, a former employee may sue a business, claiming that he was wrongfully fired from his job.

Family Disputes

Some court cases involve families. For instance, a married couple who desires to get a divorce must go to court to obtain it. Parents who desire to set up an arrangement for the shared custody of their kids—such as which parent may see the child on which days, and which parent will spend certain holidays with the child—also seek the assistance of the courts.

Civil Rights

The U.S. Constitution and the **Bill of Rights**—the first ten Amendments to the Constitution—provide several important rights, freedoms, and protections to citizens. A right is a claim or title that you are due. It is a legal guarantee.

Some of those fundamental rights include freedoms of expression and religion under the First Amendment and the right to due process and equal protection of the law, among others. When one of these civil rights is violated, a plaintiff who has been wronged may file a claim in court. As an example, a plaintiff may claim that her public school violated her freedom of religion when the school compelled the plaintiff to take part in a mandatory prayer.

Enzo v. Otis: The Facts

Let's look at a fictitious civil case, which we will follow from beginning to end in the remaining chapters of this book.

Enzo Smith was driving his car just past 7 p.m. on a Thursday evening, after leaving work at his part-time job. Enzo worked as a pizza delivery driver from 3 p.m. to 7 p.m. four afternoons per week at a local pizza shop in Anytown, located in State. Enzo was a senior at Anytown High School, and he had just turned 18 years old two weeks before.

Enzo left the pizza shop parking lot at 7:03 p.m. and drove down Main Street. About five blocks into his trip, Enzo's car was struck on the right side by another car, driven by Otis Jones. The car was going through the intersection of Main and Elm Streets, and Otis was driving down Elm Street. There was a stop sign on Elm Street, and it was not immediately clear at the scene of the accident whether Otis had made a proper stop at the stop sign before he crossed into Main Street.

Otis had just graduated from Anytown High School. He was also 18 years old, and he worked as a bank teller while attending community college in the evenings. He was heading home from a class that ended at 6:45 p.m. on the night of the accident.

After Otis's car struck Enzo, Enzo's car careened to the left and struck a telephone pole. The airbag in the driver's side deployed and struck Enzo in the chest, causing him to suffer injuries. Enzo also hit his face against the steering wheel, causing one of his front teeth to break and causing a severe cut on his lip, which needed stitches. Otis broke his left arm and suffered a lot of pain. Both Enzo and Otis were taken to the hospital. Enzo was kept overnight for observation, and Otis went home Thursday night after having a cast put on his arm.

At the scene of the accident, the police officer who responded to the accident noted Enzo's tire marks and asked whether Enzo had been speeding at the time of the crash. Enzo responded that he might have been going a little bit faster than the speed limit (which was 25 miles per hour) but not by much.

Otis's cell phone was found in the center console of his car. The cell phone was on, and it appeared that Otis had opened a text message on the phone. When the officer asked Otis whether he was reading the text message at the time of the accident, Otis refused to answer. The officer gave Otis a traffic ticket for texting while driving.

Both Enzo's and Otis's cars were badly damaged in the car accident. Otis's car needed a lot of work on its front end, while Enzo's car was a total loss because of hitting the telephone pole and the impact of Otis's car slamming against the side of Enzo's car.

Otis returned to work the next day, but he has had trouble writing, typing, and note-taking in class (he is left-handed). Enzo, on the other hand, had to take two weeks off of school and work before he felt well enough to attend. Because Enzo's employer provides no sick time, Enzo was not compensated for any of that time.

Discussion Questions

1. In the preceding description of the accident caused by Otis, what claim(s) can Enzo bring against Otis? What must he prove in order to succeed on his claim(s)?

2. What defenses might be brought by Otis against Enzo? What must Otis prove in order to succeed on those claims?

Writing Prompt

1. Which type(s) of civil cases sound most interesting to you, and why? Explain your answers fully.

_____

_____

_____

_____

_____

Chapter 15

AN OVERVIEW OF CIVIL LITIGATION

- The Civil Litigation Process
- Key Personnel in the Civil Litigation Process

The Civil Litigation Process

The plaintiff begins the litigation process by filing a document called a **complaint**, which includes the **allegations**, or claims, against the defendant regarding the defendant's wrongdoing. The defendant then answers the Complaint. The parties engage in **discovery**, which is the process of exchanging information through various documents and requests. The parties meet during a pretrial conference to discuss what will be presented at trial and attempt to settle the case outside of court.

At trial, both parties present their case by offering witness testimony, evidence, and arguments regarding legal and factual points. After the trial, the parties may make various motions and even seek to appeal the case to a higher court.

Key Personnel in the Civil Litigation Process

In the courtroom, similar to criminal cases, there will typically be a judge present, who oversees the civil proceedings and resolves any issues that arise based on the law. Judges are employed by the court, the judicial branch of the government. In many civil suits, the parties are also entitled to a trial by jury. The jury is made up of other citizens from the parties' community. The jury considers various issues based on the facts of the case and decides which party should prevail in the case. As with criminal cases, court personnel—such as a clerk, reporter, and bailiff—and attorneys for both parties would also be present during a trial.

Enzo v. Otis: Meeting the Attorney

Enzo, the plaintiff, meets with Attorney Goode, who specializes in personal injury cases such as the one that Enzo would like to bring against Otis. Enzo brings his parents to the meeting. Even though Enzo is 18 years old (and therefore of legal age to bring a lawsuit in his home state), he looks to his parents for advice regarding the case.

During the meeting, Attorney Goode consults a checklist that is specific to personal injury cases involving automobile accidents. First and foremost, Attorney Goode must get to know Enzo as a potential client and be clear about the case and the representation she will provide to Enzo. According to the checklist, Attorney Goode asks Enzo for the following information:

- Enzo's personal information and contact information
- Enzo's medical and hospital records after the accident occurred
- Enzo's records from school and his part-time job at a pizza shop
- Any police department and fire department reports or records from the accident that Enzo might have
- Any bills, reports, and records Enzo might have from the mechanic who worked on Enzo's car after the accident
- Any pictures Enzo took from the accident scene or of his injuries or damages to his car
- Any information Enzo has regarding the weather, road conditions, and traffic and road signals from the scene of the accident at the time the accident occurred
- Any documents or information regarding any prior accidents that Enzo has had
- Enzo's driving record

At the meeting, Attorney Goode also discusses the scope of his representation with Enzo. Attorney Goode explains the claim of negligence, which is the claim she would like to file on Enzo's behalf. She also discusses any defenses that might be brought by Otis in response to Enzo's claim. Attorney Goode goes over the litigation process briefly and explains the role of the attorney in a plaintiff's case. She also discusses her attorney fees, and Enzo agrees to pay Attorney Goode one-third of whatever fees he will recover from Otis. (This is the standard payment in a personal injury claim in Enzo's state. It is called a **contingency fee**, which means that the attorney will only recover her fees if and when the client recovers damages from the defendant.) Finally, Attorney Goode and Enzo sign a document called a **retainer**, in which they spell out the scope of representation and agree to the attorney fees in writing.

Discussion Questions

1. Supreme Court Justice Oliver Wendell Holmes once said that "the great thing in this world is not so much where we stand as in what direction we are going." What does this quote mean in the context of the law and the doctrine of precedence?

2. Consult the above checklist used by Attorney Goode during her meeting with Enzo. Is there anything else you would add to this list? If so, what? If not, why?

Writing Prompts

1. Write about the following: The one job I would like to have during a trial is _____ because...

_____

_____

_____

_____

_____

2. If you were representing a party in a civil case, would you want to represent the plaintiff or the defendant? Why?

_____

_____

_____

_____

_____

Agreeme

This Agr

Chapter 16

RESOLVING A CASE OUTSIDE OF COURT

- Alternative Dispute Resolution Methods

- Settlement

By now, you have learned about litigation, which is the process of resolving a dispute in court. But not every case that is filed in court gets decided in court. In addition, many disputes are never even filed as lawsuits but are instead resolved outside of court.

Alternative Dispute Resolution Methods

Alternative dispute resolution methods exist for parties who can work out their differences without involving the court system. As an example, the parties to a dispute may see a mediator, or an arbitrator, who will allow each party to explain his or her argument. During **mediation** or

arbitration, the mediator listens to both sides and allows the parties to discuss their issues in hopes of working out their differences outside of court. Some mediators are like judges, in that they are able and entrusted to make a final decision on the disputed matter. Other types of mediation are nonbinding, which means that the parties enter mediation out of their own preference and hope to work out the dispute on their own.

Settlement

Once a suit is filed in court, it can still be resolved outside of court by a process called **settlement**. When the parties settle a case, they work out the details of what each party will receive and what each will give up, and typically they agree not to go to court.

Alternative dispute resolution methods are important to the American justice system. For starters, court cases can be time consuming, so working out disputes outside of court can save the parties time. Also, court cases require the presence of many people, from attorneys to judge to jury to court personnel, which can make things much more costly for the parties and for society. Collectively, we have a vested interest in encouraging parties to work out their disputes outside of court.

Enzo v. Otis: Discussing Settlement

Soon after Attorney Goode meets with Enzo, she contacts Otis, who has also retained an attorney in the accident. Attorney Goode sends Otis's attorney, Attorney Stone, a letter that details Enzo's potential negligence claim against Otis and explains what damages Enzo is seeking from Otis.

Attorney Goode and Attorney Stone hold a conference call over the phone. Attorney Stone details Enzo's role in the accident and maintains that Enzo was partially responsible for the crash and the damages that resulted. Attorney Stone then offers a settlement—a monetary amount for the damages that Otis is willing to pay to Enzo. In return, Attorney Goode would sign a release, which would mean that Enzo could not file a lawsuit against Otis.

Attorney Goode then calls Enzo to discuss the other party's proposed settlement. Enzo and Attorney Goode agree not to accept the other party's offer for settlement, and instead to file a claim in court, because the settlement offer would not cover all of the damages that Enzo has suffered. Attorney Goode calls Attorney Stone to reject Otis's offer.

Discussion Questions

1. Why is alternative dispute resolution an important part of the American justice system?

2. Can you think of any examples of cases in which alternative dispute resolution is a more successful idea than going to court? Explain your answers.

Writing Prompts

1. A married couple needs help discussing their separation. The couple has two small children. You are a mediator, and the couple consults you for help. Make a list of questions you will ask the couple during your first meeting.

_____

_____

_____

_____

_____

_____

2. A consumer has purchased an expensive tablet computer, which has stopped working properly. When the consumer sued the company that makes the tablet, the company claimed the tablet stopped working because the consumer was using it improperly. The company sought to go to arbitration, and the consumer agreed. You are the arbitrator who has been assigned to work on the case. Make a list of potential solutions you would recommend to the parties to help resolve the matter.

_____

_____

_____

_____

_____

_____

Chapter 17

JURISDICTION AND REMEDIES

- Federal and State Courts
- Types of Specialized Courts
- Jurisdiction Over the Person
- Damages
- Injunctions

Once a plaintiff has decided to go to court, it is important to establish first which court is the right place for that plaintiff to bring his or her case. The court must have proper **jurisdiction**—that means it must have the power to decide the type of case the plaintiff brings and the power to make sure it can enforce its judgment against the defendant.

Federal and State Courts

As you learned in Chapter 2, federal and state laws can differ, and each state can make its own laws (within limits of the Constitution and other federal laws). As a result, federal and state courts often have jurisdiction over different types of cases.

In federal court, the plaintiff can bring his or her suit when the case deals with a federal issue or federal law. For example, copyrights are protected by federal statutes. So, if a plaintiff alleges that his copyright has been violated by the defendant, the plaintiff may seek to go to federal court based on federal law.

There is also something called *diversity of citizenship jurisdiction*. This gives the federal court the power to hear a case where the plaintiff and defendant are from different states. For example, if the plaintiff is from Massachusetts and the defendant is from Rhode Island, and the two parties have a serious car accident, the plaintiff can go to federal court. In order to do so, the plaintiff will have to prove that his or her money damages as a result of the accident are more than $75,000, because this is an additional requirement for diversity of citizenship.

State courts can hear all kinds of matters. Many of the claims discussed in Chapter 1 are good examples: a negligence claim, for instance, which deals with a slip-and-fall accident, or a claim for breach of contract.

The U.S. Courts website (http://www .uscourts.gov/educational-resources/get -informed/federal-court-basics/cases-federal -state-courts.aspx) has the following table to show the types of cases that may be heard by federal and state courts:

State Courts	Federal Courts	State or Federal Courts
Crimes under state legislation	Crimes under statutes enacted by Congress	Crimes punishable under both federal and state law
State constitutional issues and cases involving state laws or regulations	Most cases involving federal laws or regulations (for example: tax, Social Security, broadcasting, civil rights)	Federal constitutional issues
Family law issues		Certain civil rights claims
Real property issues	Matters involving interstate and international commerce, including airline and railroad regulation	"Class action" cases
Most private contract disputes (except those resolved under bankruptcy law)		Environmental regulations
	Cases involving **securities** and **commodities** regulation, including takeover of publicly held corporations	Certain disputes involving federal law
Most issues involving the regulation of trades and professions		
Most professional **malpractice** issues	**Admiralty** cases	
	International trade law matters	
Most issues involving the internal governance of business associations, such as partnerships and corporations	**Patent**, copyright, and other intellectual property issues	
Most personal injury lawsuits	Cases involving rights under treaties, foreign states, and foreign nationals	
Most workers' injury claims	State law disputes when "diversity of citizenship" exists	
Probate and inheritance matters	**Bankruptcy** matters	
Most traffic violations and registration of motor vehicles	Disputes between states	
	Habeas corpus actions	
	Traffic violations and other misdemeanors occurring on certain federal property	

Types of Specialized Courts

There are also various specialized courts, which can hear only certain types of cases. For example, many states have a family court, which hears family disputes such as divorce or custody matters. Many states also have housing courts and land courts regarding property issues. On the federal side, there is a court that hears solely bankruptcy cases, and another court that hears only tax cases.

Jurisdiction Over the Person

Not only does the plaintiff need to make sure that a court has jurisdiction to hear a certain type of case, but she also must file her claim in a court that has jurisdiction over a defendant.

Picture this: You live in New York, and you work and study in New York. Someone alleges that you caused a car accident. That person wants to sue you in a state court in Hawaii. Is it fair that you must go to Hawaii to answer that lawsuit against you? Clearly, it is not. In order for that plaintiff to bring you into court, the plaintiff must do so in a place where you can reasonably expect to be sued—in this case, in New York.

This concept is called **personal jurisdiction**. It describes the court's power to make the defendant answer a lawsuit and enforce its judgment against the defendant. In order for a court to have personal jurisdiction, there must be "minimum contacts" between the defendant and the state in which the court is located. As some examples, the court may have jurisdiction over a person who lives in a state, who works in a state, or who studies in a state. There are also instances where the court may use its "long-arm" laws to get a defendant into court. These laws let local courts exercise personal jurisdiction on a defendant and hear a case against them even though they're out of regular jurisdiction—for example, where the defendant sells a defective product or causes an accident in one state, but lives in another.

Damages

Damages are the monetary **remedies** that the plaintiff seeks in court. Damages seek to compensate the plaintiff for his or her losses. In the instance of an accident, a plaintiff may seek damages for the cost of medical bills, lost wages resulting from missing work, and repairs of the damage to the plaintiff's car.

Some types of damages are not easy to calculate. For example, a plaintiff may seek damages for pain and suffering as a result of the accident. As another example, if the plaintiff were to lose function, such as by having a severe injury to the arms, then the plaintiff may recover for the loss of that function, whether in future employment or the loss of enjoyment of the plaintiff's life. These types of damages are determined and calculated by the jury.

Injunctions

There are certain claims where simply being compensated is not going to make the plaintiff happy. Say, for example, that a plaintiff is being bullied by a defendant. Will the plaintiff be satisfied with a judgment of money damages? Probably not. Rather, the plaintiff would like to see the bullying stop. For these instances, the court affords a remedy called an injunction.

An **injunction** is where the court orders the defendant to do something (such as perform according to a contract) or not to do something (such as stop bullying, like in the example above). In evaluating a plaintiff's request for an injunction, the court looks at the personal rights of the plaintiff and the defendant.

Enzo v. Otis: Choosing the Proper Court

As you know, Enzo's claim against Otis is a claim of negligence. This is typically a state claim, and therefore it must be brought in state court. Attorney Goode briefly considers whether Enzo's claim could be brought in federal court. There are no federal laws involved, and diversity of citizenship does not apply because both Enzo and Otis are residents of the same state. Attorney Goode files the case in State's District Court, which is the trial-level court in which civil cases begin.

Discussion Questions

1. What types of cases can be heard in federal court? What types of cases can be heard in state courts? How are these cases different?

2. Why is it necessary to have the option of injunctions in court? Why are money damages sometimes not enough?

Writing Prompts

1. Write about three examples of situations where an injunction would be more appropriate than money damages.

_____

_____

_____

_____

_____

_____

2. Why is it necessary to ensure that a court have proper jurisdiction over the person? Why is it not feasible for a plaintiff to be able to sue a defendant in any court?

_____

_____

_____

_____

_____

TEST

Multiple Choice Questions:

Circle the correct answer.

1. Which of the following is a term for a civil or private wrong?

   A. Tort
   B. Contract
   C. Property
   D. Settlement

2. Which of the following is an example of a tort where the defendant can be held strictly liable for his or her conduct, even if no intent or fault is proven?

   A. Negligence
   B. Assault
   C. Battery
   D. Product liability

3. The person whose role is to record court proceedings is called:

   A. Clerk
   B. Stenographer
   C. Judge
   D. Bailiff

4. Which of the following is a type of civil claim?

   A. False imprisonment
   B. Contract disputes
   C. Family law disputes
   D. All of the above

5. Courts look at cases that were previously decided when analyzing a newly brought case. This process is called:

   A. Litigation
   B. Precedence
   C. Enacted law
   D. Negligence

6. Which of the following documents is filed in court by the defendant?

    A. Claim
    B. Complaint
    C. Answer
    D. Ruling

7. What is the term for a remedy whereby the court orders a defendant to stop doing something?

    A. Claim
    B. Complaint
    C. Injunction
    D. Damages

8. What is the proper term for a system of government in which power is purposely divided?

    A. Judiciary
    B. Precedent
    C. Federalism
    D. Plaintiff

9. Which types of courts hear family law matters?

    A. State courts
    B. Federal courts
    C. Both state and federal courts
    D. Neither state nor federal courts

10. What does litigation mean?

    A. A nonmonetary remedy
    B. The process of resolving a dispute in court
    C. Previous cases that the court looks at in deciding a new case
    D. The party who initiates the lawsuit

True or False Questions:

Circle the correct answer.

1. A civil claim may never be brought against a business. T   F

2. Judges work in the executive branch of the government. T   F

3. Each state has one level of court. T   F

4. Civil disputes can only be decided in court through formal litigation. T   F

5. Money damages are usually decided by a jury. T   F

6. Diversity of citizenship cases involve a minimum monetary amount of damages. T   F

7. The U.S. Supreme Court hears many different cases each year. T   F

8. Both common law (such as court opinions) and enacted law (such as statutes and ordinances) play an important part in the American system of justice. T   F

9. Mediators only listen to one party's argument in a dispute. T   F

10. Alternative dispute resolution methods are important to the American justice system. T   F

Short Answer Questions:

1. Describe briefly how a case goes from the trial level to the highest level of court.

_____

_____

_____

_____

_____

_____

2. Explain the concept of jurisdiction.

_____

_____

_____

_____

_____

_____

3. Explain the doctrine of precedence.

_____

_____

_____

_____

_____

_____

Chapter 18

BEGINNING A CASE IN COURT

- The Complaint
- Service of Process
- The Answer
- Other Important Filings

The time has begun to start a case in court. The first documents that are filed in the case are called **pleadings**. Pleadings are the documents filed by the parties that describe the parties' claims and defenses. Essentially, pleadings are the documents that explain each party's positions to the court and the other party.

The Complaint

The first pleading is called the **complaint**. The complaint is the document that starts off the litigation. The plaintiff files the complaint in court. This document details the following:

- The basis for the court's jurisdiction
- The identities of the plaintiff and defendant
- The plaintiff's claims against the defendant
- The remedy the plaintiff seeks
- The signature of the plaintiff, along with the plaintiff's attorney, if he or she has one

Following is a sample complaint in the matter of *Enzo v. Otis*:

STATE

COUNTY OF MAYFLOWER   DISTRICT COURT

DOCKET NO. 1234CV

_____)

ENZO SMITH,   )

Plaintiff   )

v.   )   COMPLAINT

OTIS JONES,   )   AND JURY TRIAL REQUEST

Defendant   )

_____)

I. PARTIES

1. The plaintiff, Enzo Smith, is a natural person who resides at 123 Main Street in Anytown, County of Mayflower, State.

2. The defendant, Otis Jones, is a natural person who resides at 456 Elm Avenue in Anytown, County of Mayflower, State.

II. FACTS

3. On or about November 1, 2013, at just past 7 p.m., the defendant Otis Jones struck the car of the plaintiff, Enzo Smith, while driving on a public way in Anytown, State.

4. The plaintiff Enzo Smith suffered extensive injuries to his person, along with damage to his automobile.

III. CLAIM

5. The defendant negligently operated his vehicle on a public way. As a direct and proximate result of the defendant's negligent operation of his vehicle, the plaintiff suffered damages.

WHEREFORE, the plaintiff, Enzo Smith, prays that:

1. This Court find for the plaintiff on the above-captioned Count of negligence; and

2. This Court afford such other relief as it deems necessary.

JURY DEMAND

The plaintiff, Enzo Smith, hereby demands a trial by jury on all issues so triable.

ENZO SMITH, Plaintiff,

By his attorney,

_____

Jayne Goode

Service of Process

After filing the complaint, the plaintiff must ensure that the defendant becomes aware of the plaintiff's lawsuit. This is accomplished by a process called **service of process**. The plaintiff must send to the defendant a copy of the complaint, along with a document called a summons. The **summons** orders the defendant to come to court and answer the plaintiff's allegations. In many states, the documents are delivered by a special law enforcement person called a sheriff or constable.

Following is an example of the summons in the case of *Enzo v. Otis*:

STATE

COUNTY OF MAYFLOWER   DISTRICT COURT

                                                      DOCKET NO. 1234CV

_____)

ENZO SMITH,   )

Plaintiff   )

v.   )   SUMMONS

OTIS JONES,   )

Defendant   )

_____)

NOTICE TO DEFENDANT—You need not appear personally in court to answer the complaint, but if you claim to have a defense, either you or your attorney must serve a copy of your written answer within 20 days as specified herein and also file the original in the Clerk's Office.

SUMMONS

To the above-named Defendant:

You are hereby summoned and required to serve upon _____, plaintiff's attorney, whose address is _____, an answer to the complaint which is herewith served upon you, within 20 days after service of this summons upon you, exclusive of the day of service. If you fail to do so, judgment by default will be taken against you for the relief demanded in the complaint. You are also required to file your answer to the complaint in the office of the Clerk of this court at Anytown either before service upon plaintiff's attorney or within a reasonable time thereafter.

Unless otherwise provided by applicable court rules, your answer must state as a counterclaim any claim which you may have against the plaintiff which arises out of the transaction or occurrence that is the subject matter of the plaintiff's claim or you will thereafter be barred from making such claim in any other action.

Witness, _____ at Anytown, the _____ day of _____, in the year of our Lord two thousand and _____.

_____

       Clerk/Magistrate

PROOF OF SERVICE OF PROCESS

I hereby certify and return that on _____, 20__, I served a copy of the within summons, together with a copy of the complaint in this action, upon the within-named defendant, in the following manner:

_____

_____

Dated: _____, 20__. _____

The Answer

Once the defendant receives service of process, he or she must answer the plaintiff's claims. The defendant's **answer** is another pleading, a document in which the defendant lists any defenses to the plaintiff's claims and admits or denies the plaintiff's claims as appropriate. Each of the plaintiff's claims are denied or admitted by the defendant. The defendant might also state that he or she lacks information regarding a certain claim, if this is the case.

In addition, the defendant's answer might contain various defenses. There are certain defenses to certain claims: For instance, in the matter of a negligence claim, the defendant might have a comparative negligence defense. There are also affirmative defenses that might apply to any claim. One example is the **statute of limitations**, where the defendant claims that the plaintiff failed to bring his or her claim in a timely manner. The statute of limitations governs the time period by which the plaintiff must state a claim. For example, if the statute of limitations on a negligence claim is three years from when the negligence occurs, then the plaintiff must bring that claim before the three-year deadline expires.

Following is a sample answer in the matter of *Enzo v. Otis*:

COUNTY OF MAYFLOWER

DISTRICT COURT

DOCKET NO. 1234CV

_____   )

ENZO SMITH,   )

Plaintiff   )

v.   )   ANSWER

OTIS JONES,   )

Defendant   )

_____   )

THE DEFENDANT'S ANSWER, COUNTERCLAIM AND JURY CLAIM

Now comes the defendant, Otis Jones, and hereby answers the plaintiff's complaint as follows:

ANSWER TO PLAINTIFF'S COMPLAINT:

The defendant, Jones, responds to the allegations contained in the plaintiff's complaint, paragraph by paragraph, as follows:

I.   PARTIES

1.   The defendant is without sufficient information or belief to either admit or deny the allegations contained in paragraph 1 of the plaintiff's complaint and calls upon the plaintiff to prove the same.

2.   The defendant admits the allegations contained in paragraph 2 of the plaintiff's complaint.

II. FACTS

3.   The defendant is without sufficient information or belief to either admit or deny the allegations contained in paragraph 3 of the plaintiff's complaint and calls upon the plaintiff to prove the same.

4.   The defendant is without sufficient information or belief to either admit or deny the allegations contained in paragraph 4 of the plaintiff's complaint and calls upon the plaintiff to prove the same.

III. CLAIM:

5.   The defendant denies the allegations stated contained in paragraph 5 of the plaintiff's complaint and calls upon the plaintiff to prove the same.

AFFIRMATIVE DEFENSE

The plaintiff was negligent in his operation of his own vehicle on a public way, which negligence was greater than the defendant's negligence. Therefore, the plaintiff is not entitled to recover from the defendant.

WHEREFORE, the defendant and plaintiff in counterclaim, Otis Jones, prays that:

1. This Court find for Otis Jones on the above-captioned Counterclaim of negligence; and

2. This Court afford such other relief as it deems necessary.

JURY DEMAND

The defendant, Otis Jones, hereby demands a trial by jury on all issues so triable.

OTIS JONES, Defendant,

By his attorney,

_____

Carol Stone

If the defendant fails to answer the plaintiff's claims, he might be found in default, which means the plaintiff will receive a judgment in his or her favor. This is called a *default judgment*.

Other Important Filings

Some other documents may be filed by the parties to a lawsuit. For example, the defendant may file a *counterclaim* against the plaintiff, stating that the plaintiff is in fact liable for injuries suffered by the defendant. In an accident, for example, the defendant might admit that he was going slightly above the speed limit, but at the same time claim that the plaintiff ran through a red light, and that was the actual cause of the collision between the parties. This claim would be brought as a counterclaim by the defendant against the plaintiff. One example is included above: In Otis's answer, there is a counterclaim for negligence against Enzo, the plaintiff.

There might also be potential claims against two different defendants, which are called *cross-claims*. Finally, it is possible for a party to bring into the litigation a third party who has not yet been sued. This could perhaps be an insurance company, a product manufacturer, or some other person or entity who is also at fault. This process is called an *impleader* and is also known as third-party practice.

Discussion Questions

1. What are the purposes and functions of service of process? Why is it an important part of the American justice system?

2. Was there anything in the sample documents in this chapter that surprised you? Explain your answer.

Writing Prompts

1. You are the attorney for a new client who was recently in a bad car accident. The client wants to know what you will need to put into her complaint. Explain in writing the components of a valid complaint. Use proper letter format.

_____

_____

_____

_____

_____

2. Now switch sides. You are representing a defendant in a negligence claim. Make a list of items that may be included in your answer.

_____

_____

_____

_____

_____

Chapter 19

INFORMATION GATHERING

- Gathering Facts
- Informal Witness Interviews
- Formal Discovery Methods

Gathering Facts

Once the lawsuit is filed and the pleadings are all exchanged properly, the next important step in the case is fact-gathering. The facts of the case tell us what happened—what caused the problem that led up to the litigation?

The attorneys for both parties must ensure that they work diligently to uncover all of the significant facts in the case before they go to trial. For example, in an automobile accident case, the attorneys must find out from their clients several factual matters. The following are just a few examples:

- The speed of the client's car at the time of the accident

- The direction in which the client was traveling
- The weather at the time
- The visibility at the time
- The road conditions at the time
- Whether anything distracted the client at the time of the impact
- Whether the client was using a cell phone at the time of the impact
- Whether the client was under the influence of alcohol, medications, or other substances while driving

Informal Witness Interviews

Much of this information is pieced together by interviewing the client, but some of it will also require the attorney to consult with other sources. For example, in an accident claim, the attorney might use the police report to gain a sense of what happened. Witnesses to the accident are also invaluable sources of facts. A witness who observed the accident can tell the attorney information that the client might not have, or can share a different perspective from the client's recall of the events.

Formal Discovery Methods

In some cases, the attorney needs information from the other party, but the other party is not likely to want to share information with his or her opponent. To ensure that the playing field is level and that each party has access to all essential information, a formal process called discovery takes place. **Discovery** is the formal exchange of information between the parties.

Information is exchanged through several methods of discovery. For example, a document called Interrogatories contains questions provided by one party to the other. If a party is seeking certain documents, he or she can send the opposing side a document called Request for the Production of Documents. A party may also seek to interview the other party or a witness under oath; this is called a **deposition**.

Parties must turn over the information that the other side is requesting, as long as that information is relevant to the case and not protected by the **attorney-client privilege**. (This privilege excludes certain types of information, such as case strategy plans, from having to be turned over to the other side, as long as this is confidential information shared between the attorney and the client.) If a party fails to turn over information that was requested, he or she can face serious punishments (called **sanctions**) by the court, such as fines, losing certain motions, not being allowed to introduce certain evidence, and even losing the case!

Following is a sample document of Interrogatories in the case of *Enzo v. Otis*:

STATE

COUNTY OF MAYFLOWER   DISTRICT COURT

                                                      DOCKET NO. 1234CV

_____)

ENZO SMITH,   )

Plaintiff   )

v.   )   ANSWER

OTIS JONES,   )

Defendant   )

_____)

INTERROGATORIES OF ENZO SMITH TO OTIS JONES

A. You are required by law to answer these interrogatories truthfully and fully, under the pains and penalties of perjury. Include all information that is available to you.

B. The court and the defendant must receive the answers to these Interrogatories no later than 30 days after you or your attorney receives these Interrogatories.

INTERROGATORIES

1. What is your full name, age, residence, business address, and occupation?

2. Was the defendant the owner or operator of the vehicle, which at the time alleged in the plaintiff's complaint, was involved in the accident in which the plaintiff claims to have been injured or claims damages?

3. If your answer to #2 is in the affirmative, state:

 a. The registration of the vehicle, giving state, number and year of registration

 b. The full name and address of the owner of the vehicle

 c. The full name and address of the operator of the vehicle

4. State, if the operator of the defendant's vehicle was a person other than the defendant:

 a. Whether or not the person operating the vehicle at the time of the accident was authorized to do so by the defendant

 b. Whether or not the defendant was a passenger in the vehicle at the time of the accident

c. Whether or not the person operating the vehicle at the time of the accident was employed by the defendant

d. Whether or not the person operating the vehicle at the time of the accident was operating the vehicle for purposes of the defendant

e. Whether or not the operator of the vehicle involved in the accident as declared upon in the plaintiff's complaint had ever operated the vehicle for the benefit or purposes of the defendant prior to this accident

5. If the person who was operating the defendant's vehicle at the time of the accident was employed by the defendant, state the usual and regular occupation of the operator.

6. State where the defendant or operator of the defendant's vehicle was coming from and where he was going at said time.

7. Was the operator of the defendant's vehicle at the time of the accident as declared upon in the plaintiff's complaint acting as the agent of the defendant and acting within the scope of his authority?

8. If the defendant was not the owner of the car, but was the operator, give the name and address of the party who gave the operator the authority to use the vehicle involved in said accident.

9. If there were any persons in the defendant's vehicle or the vehicle operated by the defendant, state the number of such persons, and their names and addresses.

10. What was the speed of the defendant's vehicle or the vehicle operated by the defendant at the exact point of the alleged accident?

11. State the distance in feet from the point of the alleged accident when the defendant or the operator of the defendant's vehicle first applied the brakes.

12. Describe in detail just what the defendant or the operator of the defendant's vehicle did in an attempt to avoid the alleged accident.

13. Describe in detail any warning or signal given by the defendant or the operator of the defendant's vehicle just prior to the time of the alleged accident.

14. State the distance in feet from the point of the alleged accident when the defendant or the operator of the defendant's vehicle first saw the other vehicle or the plaintiff involved in the accident alleged in the plaintiff's complaint.

15. How many feet from the point of the alleged accident was the defendant's vehicle or the vehicle operated by the defendant when it first came to a stop?

16. If the defendant's vehicle or the vehicle operated by the defendant was damaged as a result of the alleged accident, describe in detail the damage, to the best of your ability, naming every part that was so damaged.

17. What were the points of contact between the defendant's vehicle or the vehicle operated by the defendant and the other vehicle involved in the alleged accident?

18. What part of the defendant's vehicle or the vehicle operated by the defendant was in contact with the plaintiff?

19. Describe in detail the course of the vehicle owned or operated by the defendant, and the plaintiff from the time first seen up to the point of accident.

20. Describe fully and in detail just how the alleged accident occurred, in the order in which the events took place.

21. State any act or acts, if any, that the plaintiff did or omitted to do which it is claimed by the defendant's answer contributed to the alleged accident.

22. Describe the exact point of the alleged accident with particularity with reference to some fixed object, in front of or near what street and number, or other positive means by which the spot may be identified.

23. Did you or any agent or employee of the defendant prepare, submit or make any written statement or report of the alleged occurrence?

24. If your answer to the preceding interrogatory is in the affirmative, state:

  a. The date of any such written statement or report

  b. The substance and contents of any such written statement or report

25. State whether or not you ever made or gave any statement, whether oral or in writing, to anyone regarding the happening of the alleged occurrence, specifying in as much detail as possible.

26.

  a. At the time of the accident referred to in the complaint, did the defendant have any insurance coverage, whereby insurance will be available to satisfy part or all of any judgment which may be entered in this action?

  b. If so, specify the name of the company and the amount of the coverage.

ENZO SMITH, Plaintiff,

By his attorney,

_____

Jayne Goode

Following is a sample Request for the Production of Documents in the case of *Enzo v. Otis*:

STATE

COUNTY OF MAYFLOWER   DISTRICT COURT

DOCKET NO. 1234CV

_____   )

ENZO SMITH,   )

Plaintiff   )

v.   )

OTIS JONES,   )

Defendant   )

_____   )

PLAINTIFF'S FIRST REQUESTS FOR PRODUCTION OF DOCUMENTS TO DEFENDANT

Pursuant to Rule of Civil Procedure 34, Plaintiff hereby requests that Defendant produce the documents listed below for inspection and copying at the offices of Plaintiff's Attorney, Anytown, State, within thirty (30) days of the service hereof.

INSTRUCTIONS AND DEFINITIONS

1. You are requested to state separately for each of the following numbered requests for production which documents will be produced for inspection and copying. With respect to any document responsive to any of these requests that is withheld from production on the grounds that the document or any of its contents is privileged or otherwise not subject to production, please provide, at the time for document production set forth above, a list that describes each such document and states with respect to each such document:

(i)   Its author or address

(ii) Each of its recipients or addressees

(iii) Each person who has sent, received, or obtained copies of the document

(iv) Its date

(v)   A generic description of the document, (e.g., letter, report, memorandum)

(vi) The privilege asserted with respect to the document, or other alleged ground for non-production of the document

2. This Request for Production of Documents is to be considered continuing, and you are requested to provide such additional documents as you, or any person acting on your behalf, may hereafter obtain.

3. The term "you" or "your" means the named Defendant, including any and all of its bodies, departments and/or agencies, and any and all representatives, attorneys, agents, employees or other individuals presently acting or purporting to have acted on behalf of the Defendant and/or its bodies, departments and/or agencies.

4. The term "document(s)" means:

(a) All writings of any kind (including the original and non-identical copies, whether different from the originals by reason of any notations made on such copies or otherwise), including, without limitation, correspondence, e-mail, notes, invoices, statements, checks, check stubs, forms, applications, records, returns, summaries, books, diaries, intra-office communications, telegrams, studies, analyses, reports, results of investigations, contracts, ledgers, books of account, settlement sheets, working papers, cost-sheets, estimates, telephone records, stenographer's notebooks, desk calendars, appointment books, diaries, time sheets or logs, maps, computer data, job or transaction files, daily job reports, field reports, meeting notes, papers similar to any of the foregoing, notations constituting or reflecting oral, written and electronic communications and all drafts, alterations, modifications, changes and/or amendments of any of the foregoing

(b) All graphic or oral records or representations of any kind including, without limitation, photographs, charts, plans, drawings, microfiche, microfilm, videotape, recordings, and motion pictures

(c) All electronic, mechanical or electrical records or representation, whether transcribed or not, including, without limitation, tapes, cassettes, discs, compact discs, computer diskettes, and tape recordings

5. The term "all documents" means every document as above defined that can be located or discovered by reasonably diligent efforts. If more than one version or copy of a document exists and any such version or copy bears marking or notations which are not on other versions or copies of the document, each such version or copy is included within the meaning of the term "document."

6. The use of the singular includes the plural and the use of the plural includes the singular.

7. As used herein, the word "and" and the word "or" separately shall, unless the context does not permit such a construction, be construed to mean "and/or."

8. The terms "referring to," "regarding," and "relating to" mean comprising, indicating, concerning, evidencing, discussing, involving, or otherwise having

anything to do with the subject matter of the request in any way whatsoever.

9. Unless otherwise specified, documents created, written, used, received, sent, and/or reviewed during the period November through the present shall be produced.

10. To the extent that any documents falling within the requests below have been destroyed, lost or misplaced, please identify those documents by type, author, date, number of pages and the date and manner in which the document was destroyed, lost or misplaced.

DOCUMENTS REQUESTED

1. All documents referring or relating to the defendant Otis Jones's driving record

2. All documents referring or relating to the defendant Otis Jones's automobile insurance policy

3. All communications, correspondence, notes of telephone calls, or other documents of any kind reflecting communication referring or relating to the accident with plaintiff with any person

4. All documents which you refer to or identify in your answers to Plaintiff's First Set of Interrogatories

5. All documents upon which you relied in preparing your Answer to the Complaint in this action

6. All documents upon which you relied in preparing your answers to Plaintiff's First Set of Interrogatories

7. All documents which you intend to introduce as evidence at the trial of this action

ENZO SMITH, Plaintiff,

By his attorney,

_____

Jayne Goode

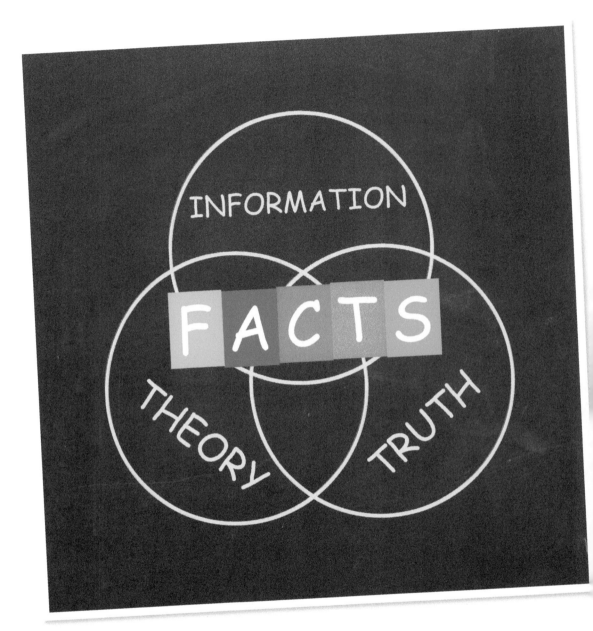

Discussion Questions

1. Why is the discovery process important? What is the function and purpose of having a formal way for the parties to exchange information?

2. What are some sources from which the attorneys can find out factual information?

Writing Prompt

1. In the case of *Enzo v. Otis*, Attorney Goode meets Wanda, a pedestrian who claims that she saw the accident. What should Attorney Goode ask Wanda? Make a list of potential questions.

_____

_____

_____

_____

_____

_____

Chapter 20

PRETRIAL MATTERS

- Motion to Dismiss
- Motion for Summary Judgment
- The Roles of the Jury
- The Roles of the Judge
- Jury Service in Federal Courts

Before the case can proceed to trial, there are several pretrial matters that the parties may bring up. A **motion** is a request by a party for the court to do something or make the other party do something. Some motions deal with the pleadings, such as a motion that requests the court to dismiss certain claims by the other side. Some motions deal with discovery, such as a motion to compel the other party to provide certain information that the party is refusing to provide. Still other motions deal with evidence, such as a pretrial motion to suppress (or keep out) certain types of evidence from the trial.

Motion to Dismiss

One motion that may be brought early on in the case is a **motion to dismiss**. This motion is brought by the defendant and claims that the plaintiff's Complaint is somehow insufficient. For example, one type of motion to dismiss is based on the claim itself—that the plaintiff cannot prove the claim he or she has brought. Some other motions to dismiss are based on jurisdiction—that the plaintiff has not filed the case in a court that has proper jurisdiction. Still others are based on faulty service of process.

Remember the counterclaim that Otis brought against Enzo, alleging that Enzo was comparatively negligent and therefore should not recover for his damages in the accident? The following is an example of Enzo's motion to dismiss that counterclaim in the case of *Enzo v. Otis*:

STATE

COUNTY OF MAYFLOWER

DISTRICT COURT

DOCKET NO. 1234CV

_____)

ENZO SMITH,   )

Plaintiff   )

v.   )

OTIS JONES,   )

Defendant   )

_____)

DEFENDANT'S MOTION TO DISMISS

Now comes the defendant in counterclaim, Enzo Smith, and claims that the plaintiff in counterclaim, Otis Jones, has failed to state a claim upon which relief could be granted.

WHEREFORE, the defendant in counterclaim, Enzo Smith, requests that the Court dismiss Otis Jones's counterclaim based on Civil Procedure Rule 12(b)(6).

ENZO SMITH, Plaintiff,

By his attorney,

_____

Jayne Goode

Motion for Summary Judgment

Another motion that may be brought before the trial begins is a **motion for summary judgment**. This motion essentially claims that no important facts are being contested by the parties, and therefore a jury is not needed. Rather, the party who brings this motion argues that the judge should rule on the case based on the law, without the need to have a jury. Either party may bring a motion for summary judgment.

Roles of the Jury

Once the case proceeds, the next step is to **impanel** a jury. The American justice system affords people the right to a trial by jury. This is the case in all criminal cases, but not in all civil cases. In civil cases, the plaintiff or defendant must ask the court for a jury trial. A jury trial is not always available. For example, certain cases involving injunctions are resolved by a judge, and not by a jury.

In cases where a jury is allowed, the jury must be impaneled, which means it must be assembled through a process of questioning by the attorneys for both sides. The court clerk calls potential jurors from the community for jury duty, which is a citizen's civic obligation to serve on a jury. The potential jurors are assembled in court and qualified by the clerk or the judge. (Among other things, a person must be a U.S. citizen age 18 or older to serve on a jury.)

Then, the attorneys ask questions of the potential jurors. This process is called **voir dire**. The questions might deal with impartiality (fairness) of a juror, such as by asking whether the juror is related to or familiar with any of the parties in the case. They might deal with the potential juror's personal feelings regarding issues in the case, such as by asking whether a juror has ever been in an auto accident.

The attorneys for the parties typically have several objections they may use to potential jurors whom they do not want to have on the jury. Once all of the questioning is complete and all of the potential objections are made, the jury is impaneled. In some states, civil cases are heard by a jury of six people; in others, they may be heard by as many as 12 people. Alternate jurors are also selected; they will be available if anything prevents one of the jurors from serving on the jury during the trial.

Roles of the Judge

The jury and the judge have different roles during the trial. The role of the jury is to find the facts: to consider what happened in the case which led to litigation. The role of the judge is to rule on the law or the legal aspects of the case. For example, the jury must listen to the witnesses and decide whether the traffic light was red or green at the time of the accident, because that is a question of fact. However, the judge decides which witness is competent to testify about the traffic light, because that is a question of law.

Jury Service in Federal Courts

The U.S. Courts website (http://www .uscourts.gov/educational-resources/get -informed/federal-court-basics/jury-service -federal-courts.aspx) provides the following information regarding jury service in federal courts.

Importance, History, and Constitutional Foundations of Jury Service

- Jury service is a direct means for citizens to participate in the judicial process. Jurors make decisions that have an impact on individuals' lives, property, and liberty.

- The jury, as an institution, has a long and distinguished history. As early as the English **Magna Carta** (1215), it was hailed as the protector of individual rights and liberties.

- In the U.S. Constitution the Sixth Amendment (OurDocuments.gov) provides for impartial jury trials in criminal cases.

- The Fifth Amendment (OurDocuments.gov) guarantees the right to a grand jury indictment.

- The Seventh Amendment (OurDocuments.gov) provides for juries in certain civil cases.

Legal, Financial, and Personal Concerns of Prospective Jurors

- Society considers jury duty so important to running a democracy that the failure to report to the courthouse when summoned can result in a fine and/or imprisonment.

- Federal law prohibits employers from firing or taking adverse action against individuals for participating in jury service.

- Federal law also provides a daily stipend for federal jurors and makes provisions for reimbursements for certain travel expenses.

- Sign language interpreters are available to deaf and hearing-impaired potential jurors.

- In order to enhance jurors' comprehension of the issues during the trial, some courts permit jurors to take notes or submit written questions they would like the lawyers to ask witnesses.

- Jurors must not discuss the case with anyone except fellow jurors throughout the trial process. After the trial, jurors are under no obligation to talk about their experience with others, including the media. Jurors also are not prohibited from talking about their jury experience. Each juror has a choice.

Reporting to the Right Courthouse: Federal and State Courts

- There are two different court systems within the United States, the federal court system and the state court systems. In the federal system, there are 94 district (trial) courts, and 12 Circuit Courts of Appeals in regions across the country. In each state, there is one state court system that has courthouses in towns and cities throughout the state.

- The federal court system hears cases based on the U.S. Constitution and statutes passed by Congress. The state court system hears cases based on state constitutions and statutes passed by state legislatures. The federal courts do not hear cases involving only state law.

What Kind of Jury: Grand Jury or Petit Jury?

- There are two types of jury systems in the United States, the grand jury and the petit jury.

- The grand jury consists of 23 citizens of which 16 must be present to constitute a **quorum** (minimum number) for the transaction of business. Grand jurors analyze the evidence presented by a government attorney and then decide, based on this evidence, whether to indict (charge) an individual with a crime. Twelve or more grand jurors must vote in favor of the indictment before it may be returned.

- A petit jury is a body of six to 12 citizens, and alternate jurors, that hears a criminal or civil case and decides the facts of the case. Unless otherwise noted, the term jury refers to a petit jury.

From the Jury Pool to the Jury Box: Voir Dire

- Not every person summoned to jury duty is selected to participate on a jury. During a process called *voir dire*, the trial judge and/or the lawyers for each side question potential jurors for bias.

- Each side has a certain number of peremptory challenges and an unlimited number of challenges for cause. A peremptory challenge allows a lawyer to dismiss a potential juror for any reason. A challenge for cause allows a party to dismiss a potential juror for possible biases.

The Job of the Judge, the Job of the Jury

- The judge and the jury have specific roles in a judicial proceeding. The judge determines the appropriate law that should be applied to the case and the jury finds the facts in the case.

- At the end of the trial, the judge instructs the jury on the applicable law. While the jury must obey the judge's instructions as to the law, the jury alone is responsible for determining the facts of the case.

What Kind of Case: Criminal or Civil— What's the Difference?

There are two types of judicial proceedings in the federal courts, criminal and civil cases.

- In a criminal trial, an individual is accused of committing an offense—a crime—against society as a whole. Criminal juries consist of 12 jurors and alternates and a unanimous decision must be reached before a defendant is found "guilty." The burden of proof is on the government and the standard is "beyond a reasonable doubt."

- In a civil trial, litigants are seeking remedies for private wrongs that don't, necessarily, have a broader social impact. Civil juries must consist of at least six jurors and the verdict must be unanimous unless the parties stipulate otherwise. The standard of proof is a "preponderance of the evidence," or "more true than not." Not all civil cases

Voir dire is French, meaning "to say the truth." This process involves a preliminary examination of a witness or a juror by a judge or attorney, or an oath taken by such a witness.

are heard by jurors; some are conducted before a judge.

- Guilty pleas and plea negotiations reduce the need for juries in criminal cases, and settlement negotiations reduce the need for juries in civil cases. Negotiations and settlements are effective avenues the courts and the parties use to arrive at justice.

Discussion Questions

1. What are the qualifications of an impartial juror? If you were an attorney who is engaged in the jury selection process, what questions would you ask to ensure that the jury is impartial?

2. How does a motion to dismiss differ from a motion for summary judgment?

Writing Prompt

1. Write a questionnaire for the potential jurors in the matter of *Enzo v. Otis*. What types of questions would you ask? Why are those questions important?

_____

_____

_____

_____

_____

_____

Multiple Choice Questions:

Circle the correct answer.

1. What is the term for the initial documents exchanged by the parties that set forth the parties' positions?

   A. Complaint C. Pleadings
   B. Answer D. Counterclaim

2. Which of the following is the first document filed by the plaintiff?

   A. Complaint C. Counterclaim
   B. Answer D. Impleader

3. Which of the following is NOT filed by a defendant?

   A. Answer C. Affirmative defense
   B. Counterclaim D. Complaint

4. Which of the following terms refers to the questioning of jurors when impaneling a jury?

   A. Motion to dismiss
   B. Discovery
   C. Voir dire
   D. Motion for summary judgment

5. Which discovery method is a set of questions sent by one side to the other?

   A. Interrogatories
   B. Voir dire
   C. Request for production
   D. Summary judgment

6. What must the plaintiff send to the defendant in order to ensure there is proper service of process?

    A. Discovery request
    B. Summons
    C. Summons and the complaint
    D. Summons and the answer

7. For which of the following reasons might the defendant file a motion to dismiss?

    A. Failure to state a claim
    B. Lack of jurisdiction
    C. Improper service of process
    D. All of the above

8. Which of the following is NOT a discovery request?

    A. Deposition
    B. Interrogatories
    C. Service of process
    D. Request for production

9. Which of the following is an example of sanctions or punishments that the court may impose on parties who do not turn over discovery?

    A. Fines
    B. Losing the case
    C. Losing on a motion
    D. All of the above

10. What motion claims that there are no material facts at issue and that therefore the court should rule for the party bringing the motion as a matter of law?

    A. Motion to dismiss
    B. Motion to compel
    C. Motion for summary judgment
    D. None of the above

True or False Questions:

Circle the correct answer.

1. A party may bring a third party into the litigation. T F

2. Informal interviews play an important part in the pretrial process. T F

3. A party must comply with a valid discovery request, or else the party may face serious sanctions by the court. T F

4. There is a right to a jury trial in all civil cases. T F

5. Either party may file a motion for summary judgment. T F

6. The role of the judge is very similar to the role of the jury at trial. T F

7. A counterclaim is filed by the defendant against the plaintiff. T F

8. The discovery process ensures that each party has a level playing field and access to important information. T F

9. The standard of proof in a civil trial is by a "preponderance of the evidence," or "more true than not." T F

10. Only a party may be questioned during a deposition, not a witness. T F

Short Answer Questions:

1. List all of the pleadings you have learned about in this section.

_____

_____

_____

_____

_____

_____

2. List five questions you would ask a potential juror if you were representing a party in a negligence claim.

_____

_____

_____

_____

_____

_____

3. Describe the purposes and functions of the formal discovery process.

_____

_____

_____

_____

_____

_____

Chapter 21

PREPARING FOR TRIAL

- The Trial Notebook
- The war room
- Exhibits

It is now time for the attorneys representing both sides to prepare for trial. Preparation is a time-consuming process that entails a lot of work, but it can pay off well, because effective preparation wins trials!

The Trial Notebook

The attorneys might prepare a **trial notebook**, which is an organized, central document with the essential pieces of information that the attorney might use at trial. As an example, the trial notebook in the matter of *Enzo v. Otis* might contain the following sections and documents:

- Copies of all the pleadings filed in the case

- Copies of discovery responses, such as responses to interrogatories and copies of documents provided by the other party
- Copies of all the motions that were filed in the case, and copies of the judge's decisions on those motions
- Copies of any letters, e-mails, and other correspondence between the attorney and client
- Notes that the attorney might have taken during client meetings, conference calls, depositions, and internal meetings about the case among members of the law firm
- Notes that the attorney might have taken regarding case strategies
- Contact information for the client and key witnesses
- Questions to ask the witnesses during trial
- Copies of important laws that are relevant to the case

The War Room

The attorneys might also put together a **war room**, which is a central place where all of the documents, important items, and preparations for trial are kept and conducted. A war room keeps all essential items together and stores everything in an organized manner.

Exhibits

Finally, the attorneys might prepare **exhibits**, which are items used to demonstrate key pieces of evidence to the jury. Exhibits often include maps (such as a map of the scene where the accident occurred); graphs and charts (such as a chart showing the future income the plaintiff has lost); and demonstrations (such as a day-in-the-life video of a seriously injured plaintiff). The purpose of these exhibits is to help the jury better understand what happened that led up to the trial. Exhibits can be helpful visual guides for the jury.

As an example, in the case of *Enzo v. Otis*, the attorneys might seek to introduce the following exhibits:

- Pictures of the accident scene
- A map of the scene of the accident and surrounding areas
- Pictures of the damages to the parties' cars
- A video reconstruction of what happened during the accident

It is very important for attorneys preparing for trial to be organized, to know where everything is, and to be able to find what they need quickly. Trials are won by great preparation.

Discussion Questions

1. What are the characteristics of an effective war room?

2. Have you ever needed to put together an outline of topics, such as the one that deals with trial notebooks? What was your plan of action?

3. Draw a fictitious map of the accident scene in the case of *Enzo v. Otis*. What information should be included if you want the jury in the case to understand what happened during the accident?

Writing Prompts

1. You represent the plaintiff in a breach of contract action. Make a list of the various sections and documents that your trial notebook will contain.

_____

_____

_____

_____

_____

_____

2. Now switch sides. You represent the defendant in the same breach of contract action. What types of exhibits might you seek to introduce at trial?

_____

_____

_____

_____

_____

_____

Chapter 22

THE TRIAL PROCESS

- Opening Statements
- Introducing Evidence
- Examining Witnesses
- Closing Arguments
- Jury Instructions
- The Jury Verdict and the Judgment

Opening Statements

The trial begins. The attorneys start with their opening statements, which convey the basic facts of their case. Usually, the plaintiff goes first. As with criminal cases, the plaintiff has the burden of proof, which means that the plaintiff has the responsibility of proving his or her case. In a civil suit, the plaintiff must prove his or her case "by a **preponderance of the evidence**." This is known as the standard of proof. In other words, the plaintiff must prove that, more likely than not, the defendant is responsible for the plaintiff's damages.

Introducing Evidence

After opening statements, the evidence is introduced to the jury. There are several types of evidence, from the contract that was signed by the parties to the defective product that injured the plaintiff. There is also testimonial evidence, whereby witnesses recall their versions of what they saw, heard, or experienced. Both sides may present witnesses. The attorney who calls the witness questions the witness first; this is called **direct examination**. During direct examination, the goal of the attorney is to find out from the witness what happened and what the witness observed. This is done through open-ended questions, such as those that begin with "who," "what," "where," "when," and "why."

Examining Witnesses

Then, the opposing attorney may cross-examine the witness. This involves questioning the witness about the statements the witness made during direct examination—for example, by asking follow-up questions about the accident scene. The attorney may also ask questions to shed doubt on the witness's credibility. In other words, the attorney may ask about information that would make it seem to the jury that the witness should not be believed. One example deals with the witness's abilities to perceive and recount information, such as asking whether the witness wears glasses and about his or her ability to see the accident from a distance. Another example deals with inconsistent statements that the witness may have made previously—for example, telling the police that a traffic light was green but later testifying that the light was red at the time of the accident.

Closing Arguments

The attorneys then deliver their closing arguments to summarize their most important points. The U.S. Courts website (http://www.uscourts.gov/educational -resources/get-informed/federal-court -resources/opening-statements-closing -arguments.aspx) explains the key differences between opening statements and closing arguments:

Each party in a jury trial has a right to speak directly to jurors once before and once after the evidence is presented. Those two sets of remarks serve distinct purposes and are governed by different rules.

- **Opening Statement:** The opening statement at the beginning of the trial is limited to outlining facts. This is each party's opportunity to set the basic scene for the jurors, introduce them to the core dispute(s) in the case, and provide a general road map of how the trial is expected to unfold. Absent strategic reasons not to do so, parties should lay out for the jurors who their witnesses are, how they are related to the parties and to each other, and what each is expected to say on the witness stand. Opening statements include such phrases as, "Ms. Smith will testify under oath that she saw Mr. Johnson do X," and "The evidence will show that Defendant did not do Y." Although opening statements should be as persuasive as possible, they should not include arguments. They come at the end of the trial.

- **Closing Argument:** Only after the jury has seen and heard the factual evidence of the case are the parties allowed to try to persuade them about its overall significance. Closing arguments are the opportunity for each party to remind jurors about key evidence presented and to persuade them to adopt an interpretation favorable to their position. At this point, parties are free to use hypothetical analogies to make their points, to comment on the credibility of the witnesses, to discuss how they believe the various pieces of the puzzle fit into a compelling whole, and to advocate why jurors should decide the case in their favor.

- **Key Difference:** There is a critical difference between opening statements and closing arguments. In opening statements, parties are restricted to stating the evidence ("Witness A will testify that Event X occurred"). In closing arguments, the parties are free to argue the merits: "As we know from Witness A's compelling testimony, Event X occurred, which clearly established who should be held responsible in this case."

Jury Instructions

Once the jury hears all of the evidence, the judge gives jury instructions, which tell the jury the law it needs to use when reaching its verdict. The jury instructions alert the jurors about what elements must be proven by the plaintiff in order to meet the burden of proof. These instructions might also address any defenses that the defendant has brought up.

Following are sample jury instructions for negligence, which is the claim at the center of *Enzo v. Otis*, along with the defense of comparative negligence.

Enzo v. Otis: Jury Instructions for Negligence

I will now give you the definitions of some important legal terms. Please listen carefully to these definitions so that you will understand the terms.

- Negligence

  It was the duty of the defendant, in connection with this occurrence, to use ordinary care for the safety of the plaintiff and the plaintiff's property.

  Negligence is the failure to use ordinary

care. Ordinary care means the care a reasonably careful person would use. Therefore, by "negligence," I mean the failure to do something that a reasonably careful person would do, or the doing of something that a reasonably careful person would not do, under the circumstances that you find existed in this case.

The law does not say what a reasonably careful person using ordinary care would or would not do under such circumstances. That is for you to decide.

• Comparative Negligence

The total amount of damages that the plaintiff would otherwise be entitled to recover shall be reduced by the percentage of plaintiff's negligence that contributed as a proximate cause to his or her injuries and damages. This is known as comparative negligence. The plaintiff, however, is not entitled to noneconomic damages if the plaintiff is more than 50 percent at fault for his or her injuries.

The Jury Verdict and the Judgment

Next, the jury deliberates. This means that the members of the jury discuss and debate the case until they reach a verdict. A verdict is the jury's decision about which party should prevail in a lawsuit. The verdict is not the final word, however. Even after the jury reaches its verdict, the judge may reduce it (a process called *remittitur*) or increase it (a process called *additur*) or even overturn it altogether! In essence, if the judge finds the jury's verdict to be unreasonable, the judge may take steps to correct it. At the end of the proceedings, the judge renders the court's judgment, which is the official end to the trial proceedings.

Discussion Questions

1. What is the difference between preparing a witness for trial and coaching the witness to say what the attorney wants him or her to say? Why is it prudent not to allow attorneys to coach witnesses?

2. Do you think it is more difficult to direct examine or cross-examine a witness? Why?

3. In some instances, a judge may be recused from a trial, which means that the judge steps down and a new judge takes over. Can you think of some reasons why this might occur?

Writing Prompts

1. Pretend that you are the attorney for Enzo, and you are going to call Wanda, a witness who says she observed the accident and saw Otis texting at the time he crashed into Enzo's car. What questions will you ask Wanda on direct examination while she is testifying?

_____

_____

_____

_____

_____

_____

2. Now switch sides and pretend that you are the attorney for Otis. What questions would you ask Wanda on cross-examination?

_____

_____

_____

_____

_____

_____

3. Have you ever observed a jury trial? Have you ever read about one, or seen one on television? Write about the proceedings and explain what occurred.

_____

_____

_____

_____

_____

_____

Chapter 23

AFTER THE TRIAL

- Post-Trial Motions
- Judgments
- The Appeals Process
- Supreme Court Procedures

Post-Trial Motions

Even after the jury reaches its verdict, the case might not be completely over. First, the parties might bring several post-trial motions. One example is a motion for a new trial. Through this motion, a party may request that the court order a new trial for various reasons, such as arguing that prejudicial evidence was admitted during the last trial.

Another example is a motion notwithstanding the verdict. Essentially, this motion says that even though the jury found for one party, the jury was wrong. Through this motion, the court can reverse the jury's verdict and render judgment for the other side.

Judgments

Once all of the post-trial motions are exhausted, the court renders its judgment. The court's judgment is the final word in the trial.

The Appeals Process

If a party is unhappy with the court's judgment, he or she may exercise the right to appeal that judgment in a higher court. First, the losing party may file a notice of appeal in the court of appeals. Then, both parties will submit their appellate briefs, which are documents that contain the parties' positions on appeal. The parties then are invited for oral arguments, where they argue those positions to the court. In most cases, the parties argue in front of a panel (or selection) of judges; in rare cases, they are heard by the entire bench, meaning all of the appellate justices who work for the court.

The appellate court may affirm the trial court's judgment, which means the justices agree with it. It may instead reverse the trial court's judgment, which means the justices disagree with it. If the parties are still dissatisfied with the appellate court's judgment, they may further appeal the judgment to a state supreme court.

In very rare cases, the case makes its way to the U.S. Supreme Court. Following is an explanation of the procedures of the highest court in the nation, from the U.S. Courts website (http://www.uscourts.gov /educational-resources/get-informed/supreme -court/supreme-court-procedures.aspx).

Supreme Court Procedures

Background

Article III, Section 1 of the Constitution establishes the Supreme Court of the United States. Currently, there are nine justices on the Court. Before taking office, each justice must be appointed by the president and confirmed by the Senate. Justices hold office during good behavior, typically, for life.

The Constitution states that the Supreme Court has both original and appellate jurisdiction. Original jurisdiction means that the Supreme Court is the first, and only, Court to hear a case. The Constitution limits original jurisdiction cases to those involving disputes between the states or disputes arising among ambassadors and other high-ranking ministers. Appellate jurisdiction means that the Court has the authority to review the decisions of lower courts. Most of the cases the Supreme Court hears are appeals from lower courts.

Writs of Certiorari

Parties who are not satisfied with the decision of a lower court must petition the U.S. Supreme Court to hear their case. The primary means to petition the court

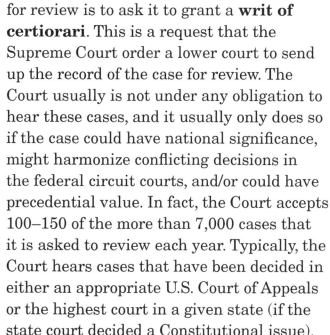

In the term writ of certiorari, the word *certiorari* comes from the Latin, meaning "to be informed of, or to be made certain in regard to."

for review is to ask it to grant a **writ of certiorari**. This is a request that the Supreme Court order a lower court to send up the record of the case for review. The Court usually is not under any obligation to hear these cases, and it usually only does so if the case could have national significance, might harmonize conflicting decisions in the federal circuit courts, and/or could have precedential value. In fact, the Court accepts 100–150 of the more than 7,000 cases that it is asked to review each year. Typically, the Court hears cases that have been decided in either an appropriate U.S. Court of Appeals or the highest court in a given state (if the state court decided a Constitutional issue).

The Supreme Court has its own set of rules. According to these rules, four of the nine justices must vote to accept a case. Five of the nine justices must vote in order to grant a stay, for example, a stay of execution in a death penalty case. Under certain instances, one justice may grant a stay pending review by the entire Court.

Law Clerks

Each justice is permitted to have between three and four law clerks per Court term. These are individuals who, fairly recently, graduated from law school, typically, at the top of their class from the best schools. Often, they have served a year or more as a law clerk for a federal judge. Among other things, they do legal research that assists justices in deciding what cases to accept; help to prepare questions that the justice may ask during oral arguments; and assist with the drafting of opinions.

While it is the prerogative of every justice to read each petition for *certiorari* himself/herself, many participate in what is informally known as the "cert pool." As petitions for *certiorari* come in on a weekly basis, they are divided among the participating justices. The participating justices divide their petitions among their law clerks. The law clerks, in turn, read the petitions assigned to them, write a brief memorandum about the case, and make a recommendation as to whether the case should be accepted or not. The Justice provides these memoranda and recommendations to the other justices at a justices' conference.

Briefs

If the justices decide to accept a case (grant a petition for *certiorari*), the case is placed on the docket. According to the Supreme Court's rules, the petitioner has a certain amount of time to write a brief, not to exceed 50 pages, putting forth his/her legal case concerning the issue on which the Court granted review. After the petitioner's brief has been filed, the other party, known as the respondent, is given a certain amount of time to file a respondent's brief. This brief is also not to exceed 50 pages.

After the initial petitions have been filed, the petitioner and respondent are permitted to file briefs of a shorter length that respond to the other party's respective position. If not directly involved in the case, the U.S. government, represented by the Solicitor General, can file a brief on behalf of the government. With the permission of the Court, groups that do not have a direct stake in the outcome of the case, but are nevertheless interested in it, may file what is known as an *amicus curiae* (Latin for "friend of the court") brief providing their own arguments and recommendations for how the case should be decided.

Oral Arguments

By law, the U.S. Supreme Court's term begins on the first Monday in October and goes through the Sunday before the first Monday in October of the following year. The Court is, typically, in recess from late June/early July until the first Monday in October.

The Court hears oral arguments in cases from October through April. From October through December, arguments are heard during the first two weeks of each month. From January through April, arguments are heard on the last two weeks of each month. During each two-week session, oral arguments are heard on Mondays, Tuesdays, and Wednesdays only (unless the Court directs otherwise).

Oral arguments are open to the public. Typically, two cases are heard each day, beginning at 10 a.m. Each case is allotted an hour for arguments. During this time, lawyers for each party have a half hour to make their best legal case to the justices. Most of this time, however, is spent answering the justices' questions. The justices tend to view oral arguments not as a forum for the lawyers to rehash the merits of the case as found in their briefs, but for answering any questions that the justices may have developed while reading their briefs.

The Solicitor General usually argues cases in which the U.S. government is a party. If the U.S. government is not a party, the Solicitor General still may be allotted time to express the government's interests in the case.

During oral arguments, each side has approximately 30 minutes to present its case; however, attorneys are not required to use the entire time. The petitioner argues first, then the respondent. If the petitioner reserves time for rebuttal, the petitioner speaks last. After the Court is seated, the Chief Justice acknowledges counsel for the petitioner, who already is standing at the podium. The attorney then begins: "Mr. Chief Justice, and may it please the Court . . . ."

Only the Chief Justice is addressed as "Mr. Chief Justice." Others are addressed as "Justice Scalia," "Justice Ginsburg," or "Your Honor." The title "judge" is not used for Supreme Court justices.

Conference

When oral arguments are concluded, the justices have to decide the case. They do so at what is known as the justices' conference. Two conferences are held per week when

Court is in session, on Wednesday and Friday afternoons. The justices vote on cases heard on Mondays and Tuesdays of a given week at their Wednesday afternoon conference. The justices vote on cases heard on Wednesday at their Friday afternoon conference. When Court is not in session, usually only a Friday conference is held.

Before going into the conference, the justices frequently discuss the relevant cases with their law clerks, seeking to get different perspectives on the case. At the end of these sessions, sometimes the justices have a fairly good idea of how they will vote in the case; other times, they are still uncommitted.

According to Supreme Court protocol, only the justices are allowed in the conference room at this time—no police, law clerks, secretaries, etc. The Chief Justice calls the session to order and, as a sign of the collegial nature of the institution, all the justices shake hands. The first order of business, typically, is to discuss the week's petitions for *certiorari*, i.e., deciding which cases to accept or reject.

After the petitions for *certiorari* are dealt with, the justices begin to discuss the cases that were heard since their last conference. According to Supreme Court protocol, all justices have an opportunity to state their views on the case and raise any questions or concerns they may have. Each justice speaks without interruptions from the others. The Chief Justice makes the first statement, then each justice speaks in descending order of seniority, ending with the most junior justice—the one who has served on the court for the fewest years.

When each justice is finished speaking, the Chief Justice casts the first vote, and then each justice in descending order of seniority does likewise until the most junior justice casts the last vote. After the votes have been tallied, the Chief Justice, or the most senior justice in the majority if the Chief Justice is in the dissent, assigns a justice in the majority to write the opinion of the Court. The most senior justice in the dissent can assign a dissenting justice to write the dissenting opinion.

If a justice agrees with the outcome of the case, but not the majority's rationale for it, that justice may write a concurring opinion. Any justice may write a separate dissenting opinion. When there is a tie vote, the decision of the lower Court stands. This can happen if, for some reason, any of the nine justices is not participating in a case (e.g., a seat is vacant or a justice has had to recuse).

Opinions

All opinions of the Court are, typically, handed down by the last day of the Court's term (the day in late June/early July when the Court recesses for the summer). With the exception of this deadline, there are no rules concerning when decisions must be released. Typically, decisions that are unanimous are released sooner than those that have concurring and dissenting opinions. While some unanimous decisions are handed down as early as December, some controversial opinions, even if heard in October, may not be handed down until the last day of the term.

A majority of justices must agree to all of the contents of the Court's opinion before it is publicly delivered. Justices do this by "signing onto" the opinion. The justice in charge of writing the opinion must be careful to take into consideration the comments and concerns of the others who voted in the majority. If this does not happen, there may not be enough justices to maintain the majority. On rare occasions in close cases, a dissenting opinion later becomes the majority opinion because one or more justices switch their votes after reading the drafts of the majority and dissenting opinions. No opinion is considered the official opinion of the Court until it is delivered in open Court (or at least made available to the public).

On days when the Court is hearing oral arguments, decisions may be handed down before the arguments are heard. During the months of May and June, the Court meets at 10 a.m. every Monday to release opinions. During the last week of the term, additional days may be designated as "opinion days."

Once all of the avenues for post-trial proceedings are exhausted, the judgment is executed. This means, essentially, that the party who was ordered to pay must satisfy the Court's judgment by tendering payment to the other side.

Enzo v. Otis: How Did the Case Turn Out?

The jury handed down its verdict in the case of *Enzo v. Otis*, finding for Enzo on his claim of negligence against Otis. The jury compensated Enzo for his medical bills, his lost wages during the two weeks he was out of work, the damages to his car, and his pain and suffering.

The jury did, however, find that Enzo was partially responsible for the accident, because he was admittedly speeding at the time of the crash. The jury found for Otis on his comparative negligence defense and found Enzo to be 10 percent liable for the accident. Therefore, Enzo's damages were reduced by 10 percent.

Otis had a car insurance policy that compensated Enzo for the damages. (It is important to note that the jury did not know about this insurance policy, nor could it consider the policy when deliberating its verdict, because it would be against public policy to allow the jury to do so.) Otis's insurance company considered appealing the verdict, but its company attorneys advised against it. The jury's verdict became the final judgment of the court and was satisfied through the insurance company's payment.

Discussion Questions

1. Why is it essential to our system of justice to have higher courts that may review the decisions of lower courts?

2. Why is it not feasible for the Supreme Court to hear all cases that are put before it? What are some considerations that the Court will employ when choosing which cases should be heard during a particular term?

3. In what ways does the law and legal system affect your everyday life?

Writing Prompts

1. Research and read about a famous trial attorney or judge. What was he or she like? What characteristics and traits did he or she possess?

_____

_____

_____

_____

_____

_____

2. It is important for all Americans to be educated about civics and the American legal system because...

_____

_____

_____

_____

_____

3. Write a handful of legal topics that you think are important. If you were a Supreme Court justice, what types of topics and cases would you like to hear, and why?

_____

_____

_____

_____

_____

TEST

Multiple Choice Questions:

Circle the correct answer.

1. Which of the following is the term for a document filed by the petitioner or the respondent in a Supreme Court case?

   A. Writ of certiorari
   B. Brief

   C. Oral argument
   D. Conference

2. Which of the following is the term for the Supreme Court justices' deliberation and decision of a case?

   A. Writ of certiorari
   B. Brief

   C. Oral argument
   D. Conference

3. An appellate court has reversed the trial court's judgment in a case. The appellate court has:

   A. Agreed with the trial court
   B. Disagreed with the trial court
   C. Granted a new trial
   D. None of the above

4. An appellate court has affirmed the trial court's judgment in a case. The appellate court has:

   A. Agreed with the trial court
   B. Disagreed with the trial court
   C. Granted a new trial
   D. None of the above

5. What officially ends the trial proceedings?

   A. The verdict
   B. The judgment

   C. The closing argument
   D. The motion

6. During trial, which side typically delivers his or her opening statement and closing statement first?

   A. The plaintiff
   B. The defendant
   C. Either side may go first
   D. The party against whom the suit is filed

7. At what point in the trial might opposing counsel ask a witness questions that might undermine the witness's credibility to the jury?

   A. During discovery
   B. After the verdict
   C. During direct examination
   D. During cross-examination

8. Which of the following refers to a central, organized collection of the most important documents and information that the attorney will use at trial?

   A. Trial notebook   C. Exhibits
   B. War room   D. Discovery

9. Which of the following refers to maps, photographs, graphs, and other items introduced to demonstrate something to the jury?

   A. Trial notebook   C. Exhibits
   B. War room   D. Discovery

10. The judge may undertake which of the following actions after the jury renders its verdict?

    A. Remittitur
    B. Additur
    C. Overturn the verdict
    D. All of the above

True or False Questions:

Circle the correct answer.

1. The opening statements and the closing arguments generally contain the same information. T   F

2. A writ of certiorari must always be granted by the Supreme Court, because everyone must have a chance to be heard in court. T   F

3. The Supreme Court has original jurisdiction over disputes involving different states. T   F

4. A witness may only be questioned by the attorney who called that witness. T   F

5. During direct examination, the attorneys typically ask questions that begin with such words as "who," "what," "when," "where," "how," and "why." T   F

6. A war room must be kept in an organized and orderly manner in order to be effective. T   F

7. A judge may never change the jury's verdict. T   F

8. Trial motions may be brought by both parties' attorneys. T   F

9. The judge gives jury instructions, which tell the jury the law it needs to use when reaching its verdict. T   F

10. Preparation for trial is time consuming but effective. T   F

Short Answer Questions:

1. Describe the preparations an attorney must take before going to trial.

_____

_____

_____

_____

_____

_____

2. Explain the process by which evidence is introduced at trial.

_____

_____

_____

_____

_____

_____

3. Explain the process by which a case is appealed.

_____

_____

_____

_____

_____

_____

DEBATE #1:

Should teenagers between the ages of 16 and 18 be allowed to serve on a jury in civil cases that involve other teenagers?

1. Introduce your claim about this issue.

   Your claim:

   _____

   _____

   _____

2. Support your claim with logical reasoning and relevant, accurate data and evidence that demonstrate an understanding of the topic and rely on credible sources.

   Support:

   _____

   _____

   _____

   Support:

   _____

   _____

   _____

Support:

_____

_____

_____

3. Acknowledge alternate or opposing claims, and distinguish them from your claim by using well-thought-out, relevant counterclaims.

Alternate claim and counterclaim:

_____

_____

_____

Alternate claim and counterclaim:

_____

_____

_____

Alternate claim and counterclaim:

_____

_____

_____

4. Provide a conclusion that follows from and supports your claim presented.

Conclusion:

_____

_____

_____

In conclusion ...

DEBATE #2:

Should children be allowed to bring a civil suit against their parents in cases where the parents have neglected to properly care for the child?

1. Introduce your claim about this issue.

   Your claim:

   _____

   _____

   _____

2. Support your claim with logical reasoning and relevant, accurate data and evidence that demonstrate an understanding of the topic and rely on credible sources.

   Support:

   _____

   _____

   _____

   Support:

   _____

   _____

   _____

Support:

_____

_____

_____

3. Acknowledge alternate or opposing claims, and distinguish them from your claim by using well-thought-out, relevant counterclaims.

Alternate claim and counterclaim:

_____

_____

_____

Alternate claim and counterclaim:

_____

_____

_____

Alternate claim and counterclaim:

_____

_____

_____

4. Provide a conclusion that follows from and supports your claim presented.

In conclusion...

Conclusion:

_____

_____

_____

DEBATE #3:

Suppose that a teenager had a party in her home and that her parents knew about the party and allowed it to happen. Suppose that alcohol was served by the teenager and that a friend was seriously injured while driving home drunk from the party, when she hit a telephone pole. Should the parents of the teenage host be liable for the injuries that were caused?

1. Introduce your claim about this issue.

   Your claim:

   _____

   _____

   _____

2. Support your claim with logical reasoning and relevant, accurate data and evidence that demonstrate an understanding of the topic and rely on credible sources.

   Support:

   _____

   _____

   _____

   Support:

   _____

   _____

   _____

Support:

_____

_____

_____

3. Acknowledge alternate or opposing
   claims, and distinguish them from your
   claim by using well-thought-out, relevant
   counterclaims.

   Alternate claim and counterclaim:

   _____

   _____

   _____

   Alternate claim and counterclaim:

   _____

   _____

   _____

   Alternate claim and counterclaim:

   _____

   _____

   _____

4. Provide a conclusion that follows from
   and supports your claim presented.

   Conclusion:

   _____

   _____

   _____

In
conclusion
...

DEBATE #4:

Suppose that a high school student engaged in the practice of cyber-bullying (bullying on the Internet) of a fellow student. Suppose that the student who was bullied subsequently tried to hurt himself and suffered serious injuries as a result. Should the student who was doing the bullying be liable for the other student's injuries?

I think...

1. Introduce your claim about this issue.

   Your claim:

   _____

   _____

   _____

2. Support your claim with logical reasoning and relevant, accurate data and evidence that demonstrate an understanding of the topic and rely on credible sources.

   Support:

   _____

   _____

   _____

   Support:

   _____

   _____

   _____

Support:

_____

_____

_____

3. Acknowledge alternate or opposing
   claims, and distinguish them from your
   claim by using well-thought-out, relevant
   counterclaims.

   Alternate claim and counterclaim:

   _____

   _____

   _____

   Alternate claim and counterclaim:

   _____

   _____

   _____

   Alternate claim and counterclaim:

   _____

   _____

   _____

4. Provide a conclusion that follows from
   and supports your claim presented.

   Conclusion:

   _____

   _____

   _____

In
conclusion
• • •

DEBATE #5:

Should every plaintiff have a chance to try every civil claim in court, regardless of the merits of the case and the subject involved? Why or why not?

1. Introduce your claim about this issue.

   Your claim:

   _____

   _____

   _____

2. Support your claim with logical reasoning and relevant, accurate data and evidence that demonstrate an understanding of the topic and rely on credible sources.

   Support:

   _____

   _____

   _____

   Support:

   _____

   _____

   _____

Support:

_____

_____

_____

3. Acknowledge alternate or opposing
   claims, and distinguish them from your
   claim by using well-thought-out, relevant
   counterclaims.

   Alternate claim and counterclaim:

   _____

   _____

   _____

   Alternate claim and counterclaim:

   _____

   _____

   _____

   Alternate claim and counterclaim:

   _____

   _____

   _____

4. Provide a conclusion that follows from
   and supports your claim presented.

   Conclusion:

   _____

   _____

   _____

In conclusion...

APPENDIX A

The Bill of Rights

The Preamble to The Bill of Rights

Congress of the United States

begun and held at the City of New-York, on Wednesday the fourth of March, one thousand seven hundred and eighty nine.

THE Conventions of a number of the States, having at the time of their adopting the Constitution, expressed a desire, in order to prevent misconstruction or abuse of its powers, that further declaratory and restrictive clauses should be added: And as extending the ground of public confidence in the Government, will best ensure the beneficent ends of its institution.

RESOLVED by the Senate and House of Representatives of the United States of America, in Congress assembled, two thirds of both Houses concurring, that the following Articles be proposed to the Legislatures of the several States, as amendments to the Constitution of the United States, all, or any of which Articles, when ratified by three fourths of the said Legislatures, to be valid to all intents and purposes, as part of the said Constitution; viz.

ARTICLES in addition to, and Amendment of the Constitution of the United States of America, proposed by Congress, and ratified by the Legislatures of the several States, pursuant to the fifth Article of the original Constitution.

Note: The following text is a transcription of the first ten amendments to the Constitution in their original form. These amendments were ratified December 15, 1791, and form what is known as the "Bill of Rights."

Amendment I

Congress shall make no law respecting an establishment of religion, or prohibiting the free exercise thereof; or abridging the freedom of speech, or of the press; or the right of the people peaceably to assemble, and to petition the Government for a redress of grievances.

Amendment II

A well regulated Militia, being necessary to the security of a free State, the right of the people to keep and bear Arms, shall not be infringed.

Amendment III

No Soldier shall, in time of peace be quartered in any house, without the consent of the Owner, nor in time of war, but in a manner to be prescribed by law.

Amendment IV

The right of the people to be secure in their persons, houses, papers, and effects, against unreasonable searches and seizures, shall not be violated, and no Warrants shall issue, but upon probable cause, supported by Oath or affirmation, and particularly describing the place to be searched, and the persons or things to be seized.

Amendment V

No person shall be held to answer for a capital, or otherwise infamous crime, unless on a presentment or indictment of a Grand Jury, except in cases arising in the land or naval forces, or in the Militia, when in actual service in time of War or public danger; nor shall any person be subject for the same offence to be twice put in jeopardy of life or limb; nor shall be compelled in any criminal case to be a witness against himself, nor be deprived of life, liberty, or property, without due process of law; nor shall private property be taken for public use, without just compensation.

Amendment VI

In all criminal prosecutions, the accused shall enjoy the right to a speedy and public trial, by an impartial jury of the State and district wherein the crime shall have been committed, which district shall have been previously ascertained by law, and to be informed of the nature and cause of the accusation; to be confronted with the witnesses against him; to have compulsory process for obtaining witnesses in his favor, and to have the Assistance of Counsel for his defence.

Amendment VII

In Suits at common law, where the value in controversy shall exceed twenty dollars, the right of trial by jury shall be preserved, and no fact tried by a jury, shall be otherwise re-examined in any Court of the United States, than according to the rules of the common law.

Amendment VIII

Excessive bail shall not be required, nor excessive fines imposed, nor cruel and unusual punishments inflicted.

Amendment IX

The enumeration in the Constitution, of certain rights, shall not be construed to deny or disparage others retained by the people.

Amendment X

The powers not delegated to the United States by the Constitution, nor prohibited by it to the States, are reserved to the States respectively, or to the people.

APPENDIX B

The Supreme Court Justices

The following justice biographies were taken from the Supreme Court website (http://www.supremecourt.gov/about/biographies.aspx):

John G. Roberts, Jr., Chief Justice of the United States, was born in Buffalo, New York, January 27, 1955. He married Jane Marie Sullivan in 1996 and they have two children—Josephine and John. He received an A.B. from Harvard College in 1976 and a J.D. from Harvard Law School in 1979. He served as a law clerk for Judge Henry J. Friendly of the United States Court of Appeals for the Second Circuit from 1979–1980 and as a law clerk for then-Associate Justice William H. Rehnquist of the Supreme Court of the United States during the 1980 Term. He was Special Assistant to the Attorney General, U.S. Department of Justice from 1981–1982, Associate Counsel to President Ronald Reagan, White House Counsel's Office from 1982–1986, and Principal Deputy Solicitor General, U.S. Department of Justice from 1989–1993. From 1986–1989 and 1993–2003, he practiced law in Washington, D.C. He was appointed to the United States Court of Appeals for the District of Columbia Circuit in 2003. President George W. Bush nominated him as Chief Justice of the United States, and he took his seat September 29, 2005.

Antonin Scalia, Associate Justice, was born in Trenton, New Jersey, March 11, 1936. He married Maureen McCarthy and has nine children—Ann Forrest, Eugene, John Francis, Catherine Elisabeth, Mary Clare, Paul David, Matthew, Christopher James, and Margaret Jane. He received his A.B. from Georgetown University and the University of Fribourg, Switzerland, and his LL.B. from Harvard Law School, and was a Sheldon Fellow of Harvard University from 1960–1961. He was in private practice in Cleveland, Ohio from 1961–1967, a Professor of Law at the University of Virginia from 1967–1971, a Professor of Law at the University of Chicago from 1977–1982, and a Visiting Professor of Law at Georgetown University and Stanford University. He was chairman of the American Bar Association's Section of Administrative Law, 1981–1982, and its Conference of Section Chairmen, 1982–1983. He served the federal government as General Counsel of the Office of Telecommunications Policy from 1971–1972, Chairman of the Administrative Conference of the United States from 1972–1974, and Assistant Attorney General for the Office of Legal Counsel from 1974–1977. He was appointed Judge of the United States Court of Appeals for the District of Columbia Circuit in 1982. President Reagan nominated him as an Associate Justice of the Supreme Court, and he took his seat September 26, 1986.

Anthony M. Kennedy, Associate Justice, was born in Sacramento, California, July 23, 1936. He married Mary Davis and has three children. He received his B.A. from Stanford University and the London School of Economics, and his LL.B. from Harvard Law School. He was in private practice in San Francisco, California from 1961–1963, as well as in Sacramento, California from 1963–1975. From 1965 to 1988, he was a Professor of Constitutional Law at the McGeorge School of Law, University of the Pacific. He has served in numerous positions during his career, including a member of the California Army National Guard in 1961, the board of the Federal Judicial Center from 1987–1988, and two committees of the Judicial Conference of the United States: the Advisory Panel on Financial Disclosure Reports and Judicial Activities, subsequently renamed the Advisory Committee on Codes of Conduct, from 1979–1987, and the Committee on Pacific Territories from 1979–1990, which he chaired from 1982–1990. He was appointed to the United States Court of Appeals for the Ninth Circuit in 1975. President Reagan nominated him as an Associate Justice of the Supreme Court, and he took his seat February 18, 1988.

Clarence Thomas, Associate Justice, was born in the Pin Point community of Georgia near Savannah, June 23, 1948. He married Virginia Lamp in 1987 and has one child, Jamal Adeen, by a previous marriage. He attended Conception Seminary and received an A.B., cum laude, from Holy Cross College, and a J.D. from Yale Law School in 1974. He was admitted to law practice in Missouri in 1974, and served as an Assistant Attorney General of Missouri from 1974–1977, an attorney with the Monsanto Company from 1977–1979, and Legislative Assistant to Senator John Danforth from 1979–1981. From 1981–1982, he served as Assistant Secretary for Civil Rights, U.S. Department of Education, and as Chairman of the U.S. Equal Employment Opportunity Commission from 1982–1990. He became a Judge of the United States Court of Appeals for the District of Columbia Circuit in 1990. President Bush nominated him as an Associate Justice of the Supreme Court, and he took his seat October 23, 1991.

Ruth Bader Ginsburg, Associate Justice, was born in Brooklyn, New York, March 15, 1933. She married Martin D. Ginsburg in 1954, and has a daughter, Jane, and a son, James. She received her B.A. from Cornell University, attended Harvard Law School, and received her LL.B. from Columbia Law School. She served as a law clerk to the Honorable Edmund L. Palmieri, Judge of the United States District Court for the Southern District of New York, from 1959–1961. From 1961–1963, she was a research associate and then associate director of the Columbia Law School Project on International Procedure. She was a Professor of Law at Rutgers University School of Law from 1963–1972, and Columbia Law School from 1972–1980, and a fellow at the Center for

Advanced Study in the Behavioral Sciences in Stanford, California from 1977–1978. In 1971, she was Co-founder of the Women's Rights Project of the American Civil Liberties Union, and served as the ACLU's General Counsel from 1973–1980, and on the National Board of Directors from 1974–1980. She served on the Board and Executive Committee of the American Bar Foundation from 1979–1989, on the Board of Editors of the *American Bar Association Journal* from 1972–1978, and on the Council of the American Law Institute from 1978–1993. She was appointed a Judge of the United States Court of Appeals for the District of Columbia Circuit in 1980. President Clinton nominated her as an Associate Justice of the Supreme Court, and she took her seat August 10, 1993.

Stephen G. Breyer, Associate Justice, was born in San Francisco, California, August 15, 1938. He married Joanna Hare in 1967, and has three children—Chloe, Nell, and Michael. He received an A.B. from Stanford University, a B.A. from Magdalen College, Oxford, and an LL.B. from Harvard Law School. He served as a law clerk to Justice Arthur Goldberg of the Supreme Court of the United States during the 1964 Term, as a Special Assistant to the Assistant U.S. Attorney General for Antitrust, 1965–1967, as an Assistant Special Prosecutor of the Watergate Special Prosecution Force, 1973, as Special Counsel of the U.S. Senate Judiciary Committee, 1974–1975, and as Chief Counsel of the Committee, 1979–1980. He was an Assistant Professor, Professor of Law, and Lecturer at Harvard Law School, 1967–1994, a Professor at the Harvard University Kennedy School of Government, 1977–1980, and a Visiting Professor at the College of Law, Sydney, Australia and at the University of Rome. From 1980–1990, he served as a Judge of the United States Court of Appeals for the First Circuit, and as its Chief Judge, 1990–1994. He also served as a member of the Judicial Conference of the United States, 1990–1994, and of the United States Sentencing Commission, 1985–1989. President Clinton nominated him as an Associate Justice of the Supreme Court, and he took his seat August 3, 1994.

Samuel Anthony Alito, Jr., Associate Justice, was born in Trenton, New Jersey, April 1, 1950. He married Martha-Ann Bomgardner in 1985, and has two children—Philip and Laura. He served as a law clerk for Leonard I. Garth of the United States Court of Appeals for the Third Circuit from 1976–1977. He was Assistant U.S. Attorney, District of New Jersey, 1977–1981, Assistant to the Solicitor General, U.S. Department of Justice, 1981–1985, Deputy Assistant Attorney General, U.S. Department of Justice, 1985–1987, and U.S. Attorney, District of New Jersey, 1987–1990. He was appointed to the United States Court of Appeals for the Third Circuit in 1990. President George W. Bush nominated him as an Associate Justice of the Supreme Court, and he took his seat January 31, 2006.

Sonia Sotomayor, Associate Justice, was born in Bronx, New York, on June 25, 1954. She earned a B.A. in 1976 from Princeton University, graduating summa cum laude and receiving the university's highest academic honor. In 1979, she earned a J.D. from Yale Law School, where she served as an editor of the *Yale Law Journal*. She served as Assistant District Attorney in the New York County District Attorney's Office from 1979–1984. She then litigated international commercial matters in New York City at Pavia & Harcourt, where she served as an associate and then partner from 1984–1992. In 1991, President George H.W. Bush nominated her to the U.S. District Court, Southern District of New York, and she served in that role from 1992–1998. She served as a judge on the United States Court of Appeals for the Second Circuit from 1998–2009. President Barack Obama nominated her as an Associate Justice of the Supreme Court on May 26, 2009, and she took her seat August 8, 2009.

Elena Kagan, Associate Justice, was born in New York, New York, on April 28, 1960. She received an A.B. from Princeton in 1981, an M. Phil. from Oxford in 1983, and a J.D. from Harvard Law School in 1986. She clerked for Judge Abner Mikva of the U.S. Court of Appeals for the D.C. Circuit from 1986–1987 and for Justice Thurgood Marshall of the U.S. Supreme Court during the 1987 Term. After briefly practicing law at a Washington, D.C. law firm, she became a law professor, first at the University of Chicago Law School and later at Harvard Law School. She also served for four years in the Clinton Administration, as Associate Counsel to the President and then as Deputy Assistant to the President for Domestic Policy. Between 2003 and 2009, she served as the Dean of Harvard Law School. In 2009, President Obama nominated her as the Solicitor General of the United States. After serving in that role for a year, the President nominated her as an Associate Justice of the Supreme Court on May 10, 2010, and she took her seat on August 7, 2010.

Sandra Day O'Connor (Retired), Associate Justice, was born in El Paso, Texas, March 26, 1930. She married John Jay O'Connor III in 1952 and has three sons—Scott, Brian, and Jay. She received her B.A. and LL.B. from Stanford University. She served as Deputy County Attorney of San Mateo County, California from 1952–1953 and as a civilian attorney for Quartermaster Market Center, Frankfurt, Germany from 1954–1957. From 1958–1960, she practiced law in Maryvale, Arizona, and served as Assistant Attorney General of Arizona from 1965–1969. She was appointed to the Arizona State Senate in 1969 and was subsequently reelected to two 2-year terms. In 1975 she was elected Judge of the Maricopa County Superior Court and served until 1979, when she was appointed to the Arizona Court of Appeals. President Reagan nominated her as an Associate Justice of the Supreme Court, and she took her seat September 25, 1981. Justice O'Connor retired from the Supreme Court on January 31, 2006.

David Hackett Souter (Retired), Associate Justice, was born in Melrose, Massachusetts, September 17, 1939. He graduated from Harvard College, from which he received his A.B. After two years as a Rhodes Scholar at Magdalen College, Oxford, he received an A.B. in Jurisprudence from Oxford University and an M.A. in 1989. After receiving an LL.B. from Harvard Law School, he was an associate at Orr and Reno in Concord, New Hampshire, from 1966 to 1968, when he became an Assistant Attorney General of New Hampshire. In 1971, he became Deputy Attorney General and in 1976, Attorney General of New Hampshire. In 1978, he was named an Associate Justice of the Superior Court of New Hampshire, and was appointed to the Supreme Court of New Hampshire as an Associate Justice in 1983. He became a Judge of the United States Court of Appeals for the First Circuit on May 25, 1990. President Bush nominated him as an Associate Justice of the Supreme Court, and he took his seat October 9, 1990. Justice Souter retired from the Supreme Court on June 29, 2009.

John Paul Stevens (Retired), Associate Justice, was born in Chicago, Illinois, April 20, 1920. He married Maryan Mulholland, and has four children—John Joseph (deceased), Kathryn, Elizabeth Jane, and Susan Roberta. He received an A.B. from the University of Chicago and a J.D. from Northwestern University School of Law. He served in the United States Navy from 1942–1945, and was a law clerk to Justice Wiley Rutledge of the Supreme Court of the United States during the 1947 Term. He was admitted to law practice in Illinois in 1949. He was Associate Counsel to the Subcommittee on the Study of Monopoly Power of the Judiciary Committee of the U.S. House of Representatives, 1951–1952, and a member of the Attorney General's National Committee to Study Antitrust Law, 1953–1955. He was Second Vice President of the Chicago Bar Association in 1970. From 1970–1975, he served as a Judge of the United States Court of Appeals for the Seventh Circuit. President Ford nominated him as an Associate Justice of the Supreme Court, and he took his seat December 19, 1975. Justice Stevens retired from the Supreme Court on June 29, 2010.

GLOSSARY

accomplice: Someone who aids in a crime.

acquittal: The verdict by which a criminal defendant is found not guilty of the charges.

actus reus: The criminal act required to find a defendant guilty.

adjudication: Judgment.

admiralty: A court dealing with maritime law.

adversarial: Confrontational, combative, argumentative.

allegations: Claims, accusations, contentions.

alleged: Supposed, suspected, unproven.

alternative dispute resolution: A way of working out legal disputes without a formal trial in court.

appeal: Taking a judgment to a higher court for review.

arbitration: A form of alternative dispute resolution.

arraignment: The process by which a criminal defendant is formally charged and enters his or her plea.

arson: Intentionally burning down the dwelling of another.

assault: Intentionally putting someone in fear or apprehension of a harmful or offensive physical touching.

attempt: Where a defendant tries to commit a crime, plans for that crime, and takes a substantial step toward completing that crime.

attorney-client privilege: The confidentiality between an attorney and his or her client.

bailiff: An officer employed to keep order in court.

bankruptcy: The state or condition of being insolvent.

battery: Intentional harmful or offensive physical touching.

Bill of Rights: The first ten Amendments to the U.S. Constitution.

brief: A legal document which sets out a party's argument or position at trial or on appeal.

burden of proof: The party which must prove its case in court.

burglary: Intentionally breaking and entering into the dwelling of another, with the intent to commit larceny or a felony.

commodities: Goods.

common laws: Laws which derive from court cases.

complaint: The formal document which begins the litigation proceedings.

conspiracy: An agreement by two or more persons to commit a crime.

Constitution: The fundamental political and legal principles of a state or nation.

contingency fee: A fee whereby the attorney is paid a percentage of the damages that the party recovers at trial.

contract: A legal agreement.

conviction: A finding that a criminal defendant is guilty of the crime charged.

copyright: The exclusive right to make copies, license, and otherwise exploit a literary, musical, or artistic work.

court clerk: A court officer who assists the judge with filings and judgments.

court reporter (stenographer): A court officer who records the proceedings at trial.

criminal plea: A defendant's answer to the charges against him or her.

cross-examine: To ask questions of the opposing party's witness.

culpability: Guilt.

damages: Money sought by a party at trial.

defendant: The person against whom a civil claim is brought; or, a person against whom criminal charges are brought.

defense attorney: The attorney who represents a defendant.

deposition: Oral questioning of a party or witness under oath.

direct examination: To ask questions of your own witness.

discovery: The formal process of exchanging information between the parties.

discretion: Option, choice, decision, preference.

double jeopardy: Being charged with the same offense more than once.

enacted laws: Laws made by the legislative branch.

evidence: Proof presented at trial.

executive branch: The branch of government which enforces the laws.

exhibits: Tools used to illustrate evidence in court.

federal government: The body governing at the federal or national level.

Federalism: A system of government in which power is purposely divided so that no one state, person, or governing body has too much power.

felony: Types of crimes which are considered more serious than others and carry more serious and significant punishments.

final appeal: A judgment from which no further appeals can issue.

forgery: Wrongful or intentional forging (copying or faking) of a document.

fraud: Wrongful or intentional deception, in which the defendant engages for some financial or personal gain.

habeas corpus: A writ requiring a person to be brought before a judge or court, especially for investigation of a restraint of the person's liberty, used as a protection against illegal imprisonment.

homicide: Unlawful killing of a human being.

impanel: To assemble a jury.

impartial: Unbiased.

indictment: The process by which a grand jury charges a criminal defendant with a crime.

injunction: Where the court orders the defendant to do something or not to do something.

insanity: A defense to criminal liability for certain persons who can prove that they did not know right from wrong when they committed their crimes.

judge: A public officer authorized to hear and decide cases in a court of law.

judgment: The judge's decision.

judicial branch: The branch of government which interprets the law.

jurisdiction (authority): The power of a court to hear a case.

jurisdiction (locality): The state, federal district or circuit, city, or town in which a court is located.

jury: Fact-finding body at trial.

juveniles: Persons under the age of adulthood.

kidnapping: When the defendant takes the victim and brings him or her someplace else against the victim's will.

larceny: Intentionally taking and carrying away the personal property of another, with the intent to permanently deprive that person of that property.

legislative branch: The branch of government which enacts, or makes, law.

liable: Found to be at fault.

litigation: The process of resolving a legal dispute in court.

Magna Carta: The great charter of English liberties.

malice aforethought: Indicates premeditation, meaning the defendant thought about and planned the killing before actually committing it.

manslaughter: Killing of a human being without malice aforethought.

mediation: A form of alternative dispute resolution.

mens rea: Criminal mindset or intent.

misdemeanor: Types of crimes which are considered less serious and carry typically lesser punishments.

motion: A petition asking the court to do something.

motion for summary judgment: A petition asking for the court for judgment as a matter of law, because no material facts are at issue.

motion to dismiss: A petition asking the court to dismiss the case.

murder: Unlawful killing of a human being with malice aforethought.

negligence: A civil claim that the defendant owed the plaintiff a duty of reasonable care, breached that duty, and that as a result of that breach, the plaintiff suffered damages.

ordinances: Local (city or town) laws.

parole: The conditional release of a person from prison.

parties: People involved in a civil or criminal lawsuit.

patent: The exclusive right granted by a government to an inventor to manufacture, use, or sell an invention for a certain number of years.

personal jurisdiction: The court's power to bind the defendant to its judgment.

plaintiff: The party who brings a civil suit.

pleadings: The formal documents that begin the litigation.

precedent: A previously established law; a standard or guide for future practice.

premeditation: Planning, calculation, cold-bloodedness.

preponderance of the evidence: The civil standard of proof.

principal: Of the first degree; the first or highest authority, the main source.

prosecution: The party who represents the state or the United States in a criminal case and brings charges against a criminal defendant.

prosecutor: An attorney working for the prosecution.

public defender: An attorney representing a criminal defendant who is appointed by the state.

quorum: Minimum required limit or number.

reasonable doubt: The criminal standard of proof.

remedies: Money damages, injunctions, or other recourse sought by a party in court.

retainer: The agreement (or fee) by which a client retains the services and representation of an attorney.

right to counsel: A criminal defendant's right to an attorney.

robbery: When the defendant steals something from the victim's body by using force or the threat of force.

sanctions: Fines or other punishments imposed by a court.

search warrant: A document which allows police to search the person, papers, and effects of a suspect.

self-defense: The defense of one's own body.

service of process: The process of notifying a defendant of a pending lawsuit against him or her.

settlement: The process of resolving a case out of court by having the parties agree.

solicitation: Asking another person to commit a crime.

statute of limitations: The time limit by which a suit must be filed.

statutes: Enacted laws at the federal or state level.

summons: A document which orders a defendant to appear in court.

testimony: A witness's questioning and answers under oath in court.

tort: A civil wrong.

trial notebook: A central document that attorneys put together in preparation for trial.

verdict: The outcome reached by the jury.

voir dire: The process of selecting a jury.

war room: A central place where attorneys prepare for trial and store essential information.

witness: Someone with personal knowledge who testifies in court.

writ of certiorari: A proceeding by which a party asks a higher court to hear his or her case on appeal.

INDEX

R

Reasonable doubt, 10, 21, 256

Reasonable expectation of privacy, 69

Reasonable suspicion, 62–63

Receiving stolen property, 39

Recklessly, 18, 33

Redress, 11

Reform, 11

Rehabilitation, 11

Remedies, 155, 256

Report, crime, 87

Reporter, court, 10, 253

Retainer, 256

Reverse, of judgment, 107

Robbery, 30, 256

S

Sanctions, 175, 256

Search
  exclusionary rule and, 71–72
  Fourth Amendment and, 68
  "fruit of poisonous tree" standard and, 72
  privacy and, 69
  warrant, 70, 256
  warrantless, 70–71

Securities (financial), 153

Seizure, 68

Self-defense, 34, 50, 256

Self-incrimination, 63

Sentencing, 90–91, 106

Service of process, 165, 257

Settlement, 146, 194, 257

Seventh Amendment, 190

Sixth Amendment, 75, 95, 190

Society, crimes against, 43–44

Solicitation, 46

Solicitor General, 222, 223

Standard of proof, 21, 193

State courts, 151–153, 191

State criminal justice systems, 12

Statute of limitations, 167, 257

Statutes, 6, 257

Stenographer, 10, 253

Stevens, John Paul, 251

Stop-and-frisk, 62–63

Strict liability, 130

Summary judgment, motion for, 187–188

Summons, 165, 257

Supreme Court, 3–4, 107, 218–227

Supreme Court justices, 247–251

T

Testimony, 13, 257

Third party, 170

Torts, 128–130, 257. See also Civil cases

Traffic violations, 153

Trial(s). See also Civil cases; Criminal case; Litigation
  civil vs. criminal, 1, 193–194
  closing arguments in, 209–211
  in criminal justice process, 90

cross-examination in, 95–96

evidence introduction in, 208

fair, 95–98

judgment in, 212–213

jury, 95

jury instructions in, 211

motion for new, 217

opening statements in, 207–208, 209–210

verdict in, 212–213

witness examination in, 208–209

Trial notebook, 201–202, 257

V

Verdict, 3, 212–213, 217–218, 257

Victims, protection of, 11

Voir dire, 188–189, 192, 257

Voluntary manslaughter, 33–34

W

Warrant, search, 70, 256

Warrantless searches, 70–71

War room, 202, 257

Witness
  defined, 257
  examination of, 95–96, 208–209
  interviews, informal, 174

Writs of certiorari, 219–220, 221, 224, 257

ABOUT THE AUTHOR

Ursula Furi-Perry is the author of ten previous books: *50 Legal Careers for Non-Attorneys* (ABA Publishing, 2008); *50 Unique Legal Paths: How to Find the Right Job* (ABA Publishing, 2008); *Law School Revealed: Secrets, Opportunities and Success!* (Jist Publishing, May 2009); *Trial Prep for Paralegals* (National Institute for Trial Advocacy, 2009) (coauthor); *Your First Year As a Lawyer Revealed* (Jist Publishing, 2010); *The Legal Assistant's Complete Desk Reference* (ABA Publishing, 2011); *Trial Prep for the New Advocate* (LexisNexis via National Institute for Trial Advocacy, 2011) (coauthor); *The Millennial Lawyer: Making the Most of Generational Differences in the Firm* (ABA Publishing, 2012); *The Little Book of Fashion Law* (ABA Publishing, 2013); and *Constitutional Law for Kids* (ABA Publishing, 2013). Furi-Perry has also published more than 300 articles in national and regional publications, including *American Lawyer Media*, *Legal Assistant Today*, *PreLaw Magazine*, *National Jurist*, Law.com, and LawCrossing.com.

Furi-Perry is Director of Academic Support and Director of Bar Essay Writing at the Massachusetts School of Law at Andover. She received her Juris Doctor, Magna Cum Laude, from the Massachusetts School of Law. She is a partner in the firm of Dill & Furi-Perry, LLP, in Haverhill, Massachusetts.

NOTES

NOTES